oodwebguide

genealogy

third edition

www.thegoodwebguide.co.uk

Dedication

This book is dedicated, with love and thanks, to my husband Jonathan, whose mother once fondly described him as a 'family history bore'. He, and earlier my father, Hubert Dingwall, have actually proved to me that tracing one's family history is by no means boring.

thegoodwebguide

genealogy

third edition

Caroline Peacock

The Good Web Guide Limited • London

Published in Great Britain by The Good Web Guide Limited
65 Bromfelde Road, London, SW4 6PP

www.thegoodwebguide.co.uk

Email:feedback@thegoodwebguide.co.uk

Original text © 2000 Caroline Peacock
Second edition © 2002 The Good Web Guide Ltd
Third edition © 2003 The Good Web Guide Ltd

Original series concept by Steve Bailey

Cover photo © The Image Bank

First edition 2000
Second edition 2002
Third Edition 2003

10 9 8 7 6 5 4 3 2 1

A catalogue record for this book is available from the British Library.

ISBN 1-903282-48-9

The publishers and author have done their best to ensure the accuracy and currency of all information in this volume; however, they can accept no responsibility for any loss or inconvenience sustained by any reader as a result of its information or advice.

Design by Myriad Creative Ltd

Printed in Italy at LEGO S.p.A.

user key

£	Subscription		IT	Italy
R	Registration Required		JA	Jamaica
	Secure Online Ordering		JE	Jewish
			NL	Netherlands

key to countries

AUS	Australia		NZ	New Zealand
CAN	Canada		NO	Norway
EUR	Europe		SW	Sweden
EI	Ireland		UK	United Kingdom
G	Germany		US	United States
IS	Israel		WI	West Indies

contents

the good web guides

The World Wide Web is a vast resource, with millions of sites on every conceivable subject. There are people who have made it their mission to surf the net: cyber-communities have grown, and people have formed relationships and even married on the net.

However, the reality for most people is that they don't have the time or inclination to surf the net for hours on end. Busy people want to use the internet for quick access to information. You don't have to spend hours on the internet looking for answers to your questions and you don't have to be an accomplished net surfer or cyber wizard to get the most out of the web. It can be a quick and useful resource if you are looking for specific information.

The Good Web Guides have been published with this in mind. To give you a head start in your search, our researchers have looked at hundreds of sites and what you will find in the Good Web Guides is a collection of reviews of the best we've found.

The Good Web Guide recommendation is impartial and all the sites have been visited several times. Reviews are focused on the website and what it sets out to do, rather than an endorsement of a company, or their products. A small but beautiful site run by a one-man band may be rated higher than an ambitious but flawed site run by a mighty organisation.

Relevance to the UK-based visitor is also given a high premium: tantalising as it is to read about purchases you can make in California, because of delivery charges, import duties and controls it may not be as useful as a local site.

Our reviewers considered a number of questions when reviewing the sites, such as: How quickly do the sites and individual pages download? Can you move around the site easily and get back to where you started, and do the links work? Is the information up to date and accurate? And is the site pleasing to the eye and easy to read? More importantly, we also asked whether the site has something distinctive to offer, whether it be entertainment, inspiration or pure information. On the basis of the answers to these questions sites are given ratings out of five. As we aim only to include sites that we feel are of serious interest, there are very few low-rated sites.

Bear in mind that the collection of reviews you see here is just a snapshot of the sites at a particular time. The process of choosing and writing about sites is rather like painting the Forth Bridge: as each section appears complete, new sites are launched and others are modified. When you've registered at the Good Web Guide site (see p. 175 for further details) you can check out the reviews of new sites and updates of existing ones, or even have them emailed to you. By registering at our site, you'll find hot links to all the sites listed, so you can just click and go without needing to type the addresses accurately into your browser.

All our sites have been reviewed by the author and research team, but we'd like to know what you think. Contact us via the website or email feedback@thegoodwebguide.co.uk. You are welcome to recommend sites, quibble about the ratings, point out changes and inaccuracies or suggest new features to assess.

You can find us at www.thegoodwebguide.co.uk

introduction

This book, first published in 2000 and now appearing in its third edition, has been an exciting personal project. Guides to the worldwide genealogy resources of the Internet continue to be produced but it is still the case that very few are aimed at helping UK-based researchers. It was, and remains, a thrilling quest to explore the vast, unruly resources of the Internet and try to sift out the very best genealogy websites, both British and international, for the benefit of UK users. Meanwhile, the resulting book is, of course, equally relevant for anyone living abroad who can trace his or her antecedents back to Britain.

As part of the updating process, I continue to visit many, many more websites than I have reviewed here, and I have again made a serious attempt to select the best and explain why they are the best. I have also deleted those that have collapsed since the last edition. If your favourite genealogical website isn't here, don't fume in silence, please. I would love to know about it, have a look at it and, perhaps, include it in one of the online updates that the

Good Web Guides regularly provide. You will find my email address listed at the end of this Introduction, so please don't be shy about using it!

I have found that there are still, as yet, very few sites where the family historian can search so-called primary data online. Perhaps, in fact, this is the moment to decide, once and for all, what counts as primary data, what is secondary and what, in my terminology, is tertiary. Primary data, strictly speaking, is original documents, such as the actual Parish Record hand-written by a parish priest. Although online photographic reproduction of such pages is becoming more common, most such records, most notably those in the famous IGI (International Genealogical Index), have been transcribed, either onto microfiches or, more recently, into a readable form on the internet.

Of course, wherever transcription is involved a danger of inaccuracy creeps in. Mis-reading of old-fashioned handwriting is only one problem. Actual mischief becomes a possibility, as is illustrated by one now celebrated case in the 1881 Census record. In this instance, a family appears whose members lived to impossibly advanced ages, fathered children either in their infancy or in their dotage (or indeed even before they were themselves born) and employed improbable servants from countries all over the globe. This is now recognised as an elaborate joke, but it explains why transcribed data has to be considered 'secondary' data.

At the next level are family histories compiled by individuals and these, though often loosely termed secondary material, are really in my view tertiary records. It is essential that the novice family historian should treat these with extreme care. When a little bit of a gap opens up in the family tree and absolute certainty can't be assured, it may become all too tempting to take just a tiny leap of faith and 'adopt' an ancestor as part of the tree without being 100 percent certain that the link is correctly made.

Some, perhaps most, family historians are extremely rigorous about checking their sources and listing them. A few are not. So if you approach a general namesearch website, and there are plenty to attract you with several good ones being listed here, do so with extreme caution. If you find yourself being offered a family tree in a one-name website or by means of a personal GEDCOM (GEnealogical Data COMmunication) file, don't necessarily accept it all as being gospel. The mantra of the really dedicated genealogist is 'Check, check and check again.'

Please be most cautious of all when you are offered all sorts of not inexpensive gifts, even from bodies so apparently reputable as Burke's Peerage. Keep your discriminating wits about you and check very carefully before being seduced into thinking that you belong to a noble line, are entitled to bear arms and should accordingly commission an inscribed pedigree complete with ancient seal – let alone have your family crest printed on wall-plaques, mugs and T-shirts!

Having offered those caveats though, there are great, great genealogical and family history riches to be explored on the Internet. All the websites I know of that allow you to consult actual transcribed records are here. So are all those, and these are in the majority, that tell you where vital records are to be found. In addition, there is also a host of enthralling websites where simply trawling around, following up slender threads, may lead to wonderful discoveries.

If we're being fussy about terminology, a genealogist is one who is seeking to trace his family tree back generation by generation, deviating neither to left nor right. A family historian, on the other hand, is captivated by the wider picture and moves out, laterally, to explore the historical or social context in which his or her ancestors lived. To cover this distinction, please note that Good Web Guides have now produced a smaller companion volume called The Good Web Guide to Family History, in which the selection of websites is deliberately chosen to overlap as little as possible with what appears here.

A few other words of explanation may be useful. When I say 'on the occasion tested...' it usually means that I have used a family name or other reference that I know should produce a result to see whether the outcome is satisfactory. I have had to make some painful exclusions from the list. It was immediately clear that there would not be room to include any chapter on one-name websites, especially as new ones are being posted daily, but only to mention the umbrella organisations through which you can find out about them. In due course, it also became plain that individual local Family History Societies and even good local records centres, like the admirable Borthwick Institute of Historical Research in York, would have to be left out too. For the same reason local and university libraries are not listed here either. I can confidently assure you, however, that the links to all of these are to be found from within other websites that are reviewed here.

That leads me to another problem, that of overlap. Many websites cover a huge amount of ground. Some not only provide basic guidance, list data resources and give details of access, but also offer online tutorials, list coming events, sell books online and link to namesearch facilities as well. Deciding where to categorise them has been difficult. In the end I have sought to situate each one in the most comfortably applicable chapter as a main entry and then refer to it again under other headings with cross-references. I hope this makes the book as user-friendly as possible.

Well, as I promised, here's how to get back at me if you don't like (or perhaps if you do) what you find here. I'm learning too, and I will be very glad indeed to hear from you.

Caroline Peacock

Email address: caroline@thegoodwebguide.com

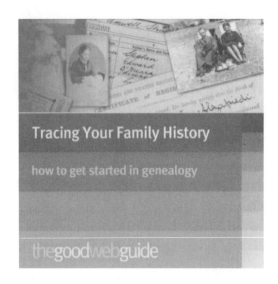

Also from The Good Web Guide

Tracing Your Family History: How To Get Started In Genealogy

£4.99

Available from www.thegoodwebguide.co.uk
or phone 020 7720 8919 to order now

Chapter 1

genealogy and the web

Ancestral research on the web

The purpose of this book is to help those who are interested either in tracing the descents of their families from ancestors to the present day (genealogy) or in building a wider picture of those people's lives (family history), by making use of the internet. Many researchers want, in fact, to build up a composite picture, taking the route of both the genealogist and the family historian. Some will already have done quite a lot of research and will be seeking merely to consolidate and extend it with reference to the web. Others will be tackling the subject for the first time.

Can I do it all on the web?

The first question many researchers ask is, 'Can I do it all on the web?' It is certainly true that there is a lot of information, both genealogical and historical, now available on the web and it is being added to all the time, but the short answer to that question has to be 'No'. Unfortunately, it is not possible, or certainly not yet, to start from scratch and build up a complete family tree using just a PC and a modem.

There are two reasons why this is so. One, as explained in the Introduction, is that there are still very few actual records available for consultation online. Much the biggest, fully searchable, online record is without question the famous International Genealogical Index (IGI), which is still being compiled by the members of the Church of Jesus Christ of the Latter-Day Saints. (It can, of course, also be consulted in microfiche form in county and some local libraries, as well as in Family History centres run by the Church).

The 1901 census has been digitised for release on the web, and further census records may soon be consulted online. The 1881 census, however, is available in its entirety on CD-ROM and the 1851 census is partially available by the same means; copies of these can be ordered online. The first census was taken in 1801 and all census records, taken every ten years, are lodged at the Family Records Centre in London. Things are changing fast, however, and it is clear that in a few years' time many more records will be searchable online and the situation will be completely transformed. Even when much larger bodies of data are transcribed, however, researchers using the web will do well to remember that they will still be consulting secondary records (records that have been transcribed) rather than the original, primary documents.

The second reason why it is not possible to do all family history research on the web is that even such material as is available doesn't come close enough to the present day. You will still need to start by quizzing older members of your family and getting as much information as you can by that means first. Documents in your family's possession may help fill out the picture. Few families, perhaps, are fortunate enough to have an ancient family Bible in which each generation's names have been carefully inscribed, but many will have other items of memorabilia, such as photograph albums, certificates or old letters and diaries from which to gain clues.

Family records

In terms of simply working out a family tree you can, of course, consult the records of Births, Deaths and Marriages (often known as BDMs), also held at the Family Records Centre, and probably travel back fairly easily to 1837 when registration began in England and Wales. Registration did not begin until 1855 in Scotland. Beyond that point you will be dependent on parish registers, some 11,000 transcripts of which are held by the Society of Genealogists. The IGI is made up of material largely taken from parish registers, though this is limited to baptisms and marriages, so is slightly less informative than parish registers, which will record burials and sometimes other events as well.

Schools and Apprenticeship records are more difficult to track down, as some are still in the possession of the institutions themselves, in local or county education offices or libraries. The Public Record Office, the Guildhall Library and the Society of Genealogists may all be able to help. Army, Navy, Police and Criminal records are also held at the Public Record Office, as are details of tax returns from the Domesday Book onwards.

It is in this sort of area that making use of the internet really comes into its own. As already explained, in most cases you can't yet read the contents of actual documents online but, most important, you can find out which documents are held where. Somewhere in this book you will certainly find a web site that will tell you where your local or county library is and which records it holds. Another will direct you to your nearest Family History Society. Others will tell you which national bodies hold records that you need to consult. Armed with that information you can plan a visit in person to consult such records, having already saved yourself an enormous amount of time by identifying in advance exactly what you want to see. Alternatively, in many cases you can make use of a service that will send you copies. Several such reputable services can be accessed online and not all of them are costly. Some will perform limited searches on your behalf free of charge.

Tutorials on the web

Another way in which you can make use of websites reviewed here is for learning more about the methodology of family research. GENUKI, for example, offers an excellent online introduction to the whole matter entitled 'Getting Started in Genealogy and Family History'. You may find it worthwhile to print off these seven pages and keep them by you as you get underway. They do deliver the warning that such notes are no substitute for 'good old-fashioned books' and, as you get more deeply into the quest, you will almost certainly find that you do need to consult books as well, but these notes are still a good way of setting the scene.

There are many other websites here that offer similar tutorial articles. It may be worth mentioning that, for the UK-based researcher, it is probably more relevant to make use of a British website for such purposes, rather than an American one. This is not to suggest for a moment that American-based tutorials are unreliable, since in general terms they will give you all the same very sound advice. However, they will not direct you to the right data sources unless you have established at some stage in your search that you are looking to consult British records (assuming this is the case). As a rough guide, URLs that end '.uk' will, of course be British. Those that end '.org' may well be British, and will be public bodies. Those that end '.com' are more likely to be American.

Having established that genealogy means going backwards in time, and family history means going outwards in exploration, where do you go next? It would be convenient if the websites on the internet fell neatly into those two categories. They don't. Many of them are not what you would call 'neatly contained' at all. With some 500,000 genealogical websites already posted and more being added every day, the opportunities for sites to assemble a multiplicity of links and become massively sprawling, all-things-to-all-men, gallimaufries of information are enormous.

Right at the beginning, the difficulty of classifying websites becomes evident. It seems obvious, for instance, that Family Search, the website that contains the IGI, should head the Searching for Names chapter. In fact, when you start consulting it you discover that it contains a great deal of other information, too, under a catch-all link entitled 'Browse Categories'. This, in turn, leads to a list of countries. From this massive databank you can review the records held in each country: a feature that earns this amazing website a place in the first, general section of this book.

Because of this difficulty of classification, do explore all the chapters here. In almost any of the websites reviewed you will find things that will either help or, at the very least, intrigue you. Some will enthral you, some will amuse. There really is a huge variety out there. I hope, having sifted out some of the less helpful ones, that not too many will infuriate you. Happy hunting!

Moving around the internet

How to move around large websites on the internet

People already familiar with using the internet, though not necessarily for genealogical research, will probably find that much of what follows is obvious. But those who have never explored the internet as a resource before may be glad of some help, particularly as so many genealogical web sites are extremely large. So I make no apology for the next few paragraphs. Those who know it all already can skip them.

First and foremost there is the absolute necessity of typing the URL (website address) correctly. Any error, however minor, will produce a 'page unavailable' notice. So the first thing to check, if there is a problem, is that the address has been entered correctly.

Once you have opened a website and started moving through it, the quickest way back to any earlier pages is to use the Back button at the top left of the page to retrace your steps. Alternatively, look for words such as 'home' or 'main' to return to the 'front' page (usually known as the homepage and always referred to as such here).

Scrolling down any given page can be done by two methods. One way is to click repeatedly on the up and down arrows in the right-hand toolbar, which allows you to move slowly and deliberately. To move much more rapidly, click and hold on the block between the two arrows and then slide it up or down the bar to the required new position and release. To move a whole page at a time, you can use the 'page up' and 'page down' buttons on your keyboard. Alternatively, clicking in the scroll bar just below the block will produce an automatic 'page down' result.

Sometimes, in the case of very long pages or lists, you may be scrolling through rapidly and appear to come to the end of your options before the list is complete. If the scroll block won't continue down the bar, you should probably just wait a few moments, during which the block will move back up the bar, to give the remainder of the page time to load.

To find a particular word or name in very large documents or lists, use the Find facility in your browser (found under the Edit menu), which gives you a search box and will find all occurrences of that word in the page you are viewing.

Clicking on a 'link' means moving your cursor to either the relevant picture or words on the screen and clicking rapidly, usually twice with the principal (left-hand) button on your mouse. The link will then usually become highlighted, underlined and/or change colour. When an egg-timer symbol appears this means things are happening, whereas reverting to the cursor arrow or a hand means they are not.

Sometimes, clicking on a link will bring up a new, superimposed window. When this happens, you will probably need to enlarge the picture in order to read all the text. You do this by clicking in the 'maximise' square, which is the middle button of the three at the extreme right of the top-of-page toolbar. Once you have made use of the new information, you can either exit (right-hand button of the three) or minimise (left-hand button). Minimising rather than exiting will leave the name of the website just visited still visible in the bottom-of-page toolbar, which means you can re-open it quickly if you need to. Exiting, on the other hand, would mean that to return you would have to open it from scratch again.

Many of the websites in this book offer a 'Search' facility. If a search box has no 'go', 'search', 'find' or similar button, press the return key on your keyboard to initiate a search. Indeed, it is often quicker to do it this way, though you will find that a few search facilities insist on your using the button provided. Some searches require you to fill a succession of boxes with information before a search can be activated. Moving through a sequence of this sort can often be done more quickly by using the 'tab' key (above 'Caps Lock') on your keyboard than by moving the cursor each time with the mouse. Incidentally, many such sequences mark the compulsory boxes, as opposed to those you can leave blank, with an asterisk or similar device.

To leave one website and move to a completely new one, put the cursor in the 'Address' box at the top of the page and click with the left-hand mouse button once. This will highlight the current address and, as soon as you start typing, the address of the new site will immediately replace it.

It is not necessary to type 'http://' each time – simply type exactly the letters that appear as the URL in this book, usually starting with 'www'. It is not normally necessary to observe capital letters, though they appear to matter on GENUKI-based sites. Simply pressing return on your keyboard, or 'go' if you prefer, will trigger the search for that website.

Once a website is open, its name will appear (probably in an abbreviated form) at the very bottom of your on-screen page, somewhere between 'Start' on the extreme left and the clock on the extreme right. If you open several sites, or windows, simultaneously, you can use these newly created name-buttons to move between them.

If a website comes up as unavailable, clicking on the word 'Refresh' very seldom sorts the problem, though it is always worth one try. Normally, it is better to abandon the quest and return on a later occasion, though do check before you leave that you have typed the site address correctly. Browsers vary in the cleverness with which they manage to find incorrectly addressed sites. If you find you have indeed made an error in the address, click on the address box twice rather than once, dismissing the highlighting, and then alter the necessary letters before pressing return or clicking on 'go' to try again. See p. 23 for further ideas.

Using a search engine to find the names of likely sites of interest is going to be one of the principal ways in which you use the internet for your genealogical researches. There are numerous portals (search engines restricted to specific fields of interest), general search engines, and meta-search engines (which search, in a single operation, the resources of many general search engines) available to you. I have my doubts about the usefulness of meta-searchers, because they normally 'present' your question to the individual search engines by means of a single, universal method, and this may not always work. They can then appear to have searched many different resources, without actually having done so. If you do decide to use a meta-searcher, one of the best is www.allsearchengines.com.

Good general search engines include Yahoo, Hotbot (now associated with Lycos), Altavista and so on. My preferred first choice is always www.Google.co.uk, for the following reasons: first, it is quick; second, it doesn't clutter its pages with advertisements; third, it lists the most likely matches first; fourth, and very importantly, it gives you a brief guide to what each website is about; and, finally, if you know the title of the organisation you are seeking but don't know the online address, you can try clicking on the 'I'm Feeling Lucky' button rather than the normal 'Search' button. Usually you will then hop to the relevant web site immediately. By the way, remember to use '.co.uk' after the search engine name wherever it applies – though if you try it with Hotbot (for which the correct address is '.com'), you will find that some canny entrepreneur has grabbed the name and is offering you furry hot water bottles!

On the whole, websites are surprisingly forgiving. If you start loading a page and, as soon as you see the first part of it, realise it is not what you want, you don't have to wait for it to finish loading completely before going elsewhere. You can use your back button or, if the index you came from is still visible, click on an alternative link before the 'wrong' page is complete. You may think this would cause a crash but in practice it very seldom does.

Many search facilities, both those of general search engines and those within individual web sites, will allow the use of some linking words, typically 'and', 'or' and 'not'. Some don't, though, and some (Google is one) assume 'and' automatically if there are two or more words in the search and inform you rather condescendingly that using it is unnecessary. In addition, some (such as Lycos advanced search) offer options such as 'the exact phrase' or 'all the words in any order'. This latter is useful when, for instance, you are looking for a name but don't know for certain how it will be presented, whether as 'John William Smith' or as 'Smith, John William'. Often, you can only find out how sophisticated any given search is by experimenting.

At various points you may be offered downloadable documents as PDF (Portable Document Format) files, that are only readable if you have an Adobe Acrobat Reader. In these instances you are normally offered the relevant button for obtaining the reader on the spot, although this free program now comes pre-installed on most computers. Clicking on an Adobe Acrobat Reader button brings up a new window, with a long list of versions of the reader, from which you select 'Acrobat Reader - Windows' (unless you are working with an Apple Macintosh or another operating system). Now you are offered a new list from which you select the most appropriate version, typically in English (either with or without 'search' depending on how much memory you have available — with 'search' it takes about 6 megabytes) and the most recent date. The next stage is to fill in a name and email address, after which you can again instruct to download. Wait for another window to appear, in which you check that you are downloading to disk, and click again.

A lengthy transmission process will now ensue, taking probably half an hour or so, during which your window will show pages 'flying' from the globe on the left into an open yellow file. Having done all this, you then have to find the file in your hard drive, going in through Windows Explorer or equivalent. It will be pretty recognisable anyway because of the large memory requirement, and will be in there under a title something like 'rs405eng'. Double click on that to 'unzip' it, and follow instructions. Now, returning to the file you originally wanted to download and read, you should have no problem.

Finally, I refer you to a very useful, relatively recently posted web site called Newbies Helping Newbies. A group of friends in Forbes, New South Wales, Australia has been meeting for some time to pool their collective knowledge of computers and share their enjoyment of genealogy. The next obvious step was to put their assembled information together in a computer-accessible form, initially just for use by themselves and others who asked. Now the Newbies have a website, which is a model of clarity and does a remarkably good job of de-mystifying both the Internet as a whole and genealogy web sites in particular. For de-bugging problems of internet use, they are especially helpful. The genealogy stuff is, of course, written from an Australian starting point, though it is still very good. See Newbies Helping Newbies at www.angelfire.com/mt/forbesnewbies/index.html.

What to do when a URL will not work

The problem for a guide like this, where so many of the sites reviewed are produced by individuals, is to keep up with all this quiet activity. URLs can be long and difficult to type as the site creators are often using space on servers intended for different purposes, and they may have to move as their sites grow too big to continue on such ad hoc server arrangements, or the creator moves jobs, or their ISP goes bust or is taken over.

If, therefore, you have difficulty connecting to any of the URLs listed, try the following steps:

• Check your typing very carefully. A misplaced dot or slash, or a rogue letter space will make it fail.

• Try connecting from the hot links on http://thegoodweb guide.co.uk/chan_gene.

• Leave it, and try again later. Many sites experience temporary server problems, particularly during busy periods.

• Search on Google (see p. 132) for keywords taken from the URL, the name of the site, the name of the creator, or from the review. This is a good way of discovering if a site has moved. And if you can't find it, it may lead you to other sites that can help with a similar topic.

Above all have fun, and enjoy the detours.

Saving time and money

A concern for many genealogy or family history researchers using the internet will be the amount of time spent online and the consequent cost. There are various ways of limiting this. For a start, of course, you may or may not be paying for your ISP. But even if you use a free provider, you are probably still being charged for the time spent online, in line with local call telephone charges. Using the internet after 6pm or at weekends is usually cheaper than during weekday daytimes. Unfortunately, of course, these tend to be the busiest times because everyone else in Britain (and more than a third of the homes in the country now have internet access) is doing the same, so you are likely to find that connections are slower and downloading individual web sites takes longer.

Once you have made a connection, remember that you have automatically spent the basic charge (currently around 4p) anyway, so you may as well make use of your time up to that value. At the best off-peak periods this may be as much as four minutes. The best way of mitigating the costs thereafter is probably to click on all the pages of a website that you think you are going to find useful, opening them sequentially but not actually spending time reading your way through them, and then close your connection. For a period, certainly for hours and perhaps up to a week, depending on the amount of memory dedicated to your cache (or 'Temporary Internet Files' if you're using Internet Explorer), you will find that you probably still have access to these areas and can trawl around at your leisure. You need

to select the 'Browse Offline' option. Even if you find that there are further pages you should have opened, it will be cheaper to go online again for a short period to do so, rather than stay online throughout your use of the site. To ensure that a page you may want to return to is not automatically deleted as your cache fills up, from the File menu use the 'Save As' option, which will allow you to save the page to your hard disk. Or you can always use the Print option from the File menu of your browser to print out a copy of a page.

If you quit, switch off and then want to return later, simply click on the down arrow to the right of your address box when you go back online and this will bring up a list of the most recently visited sites. An alternative to re-finding sites in this way is 'bookmarking' them (selecting 'Favorites' from above the address box and then clicking on 'Add to Favorites'), but this is probably best reserved for those sites that do indeed turn out to be your favourites over time.

If you find that the genealogy bug becomes life-dominating (and many have!), you may want to think about seeking not only a free ISP but also unlimited online time. It's not totally free, of course, because you do pay a join-up fee or an annual subscription. For the purposes of writing this book, when I realised that I would be racking up a massive phone bill if I didn't do something radical, I decided to link to a service that would give me unlimited online time 24-hours-a-day for a year. I found the one I am using by putting the words 'unlimited Internet UK' into a search engine (the UK bit is important). Most ISPs now offer a variant on BT's Surftime and Surftime Anytime packages that give you unmetered calls, either in off-peak periods, or 24 hours per day. Meanwhile, although I had to pay to subscribe, I didn't hesitate once I worked out that I would otherwise have spent the same amount of money using the internet within my first three days!

If you decide not to follow this route, and are consequently still paying for your online time, you may like to consult the chapter entitled 'How to Move Around Large Websites on the Internet', in the hope of picking up some tips on such things as rapid scrolling through sites, quick filling of search boxes and so on. In any case, one of the things that will be most useful in the long term is simple familiarity with the way the internet works. After that point, the next stage is familiarity with how typical genealogical web sites work, because very many of them are extremely similar in the way they operate. Good luck!

Chapter 2

essential sites

In this chapter you will find the websites of major organisations that are likely to be central to your research, as well as some smaller ones that either offer good tutorial assistance or list a large number of relevant links. Some of these websites are so extensive that it is only possible to give a glimpse of their riches. You will simply have to spend some time exploring them to discover the full range of information they provide.

The difficulty of categorisation has already been mentioned. Many of the websites listed in this chapter also have entries elsewhere, for instance, when they present online links to book or software sales, to research assistance, to libraries, or when they publish a magazine. Meanwhile, Ancestry.com, which opens the Searching For Names chapter, and other similar websites could also have appeared here. The chapter categories are a guide, therefore, and not a rigid system dividing one type of website from another.

It is also important to understand the system of ordering used for the reviews. The Good Web Guide's policy, which is followed here, is to list websites with a five-star overall rating first, then the four-star sites, and so on. Where several sites earn the same rating, they are then listed alphabetically. Full reviews may be followed by mini-reviews of sites that are worthy of mention but do not require in-depth discussion or which have been reviewed more fully elsewhere.

The star ratings relate not only to the content of each website, but also to the ease, or otherwise, of using it. Points for readability, navigation and speed are clearly issues of practical use, whereas I have taken updating, content and overall rating to be more related to a qualitative assessment of the material for the purposes of UK-based genealogical research. This means that websites that may be excellent in themselves but are of only limited use to the genealogist will rate an overall lower star score accordingly. Please don't avoid them, however, or you may miss out on a nugget of pure gold.

First Steps

www.bbc.co.uk/history/community/family
BBC Family History

Overall rating: ★ ★ ★ ★			
Classification:	General	Readability:	★ ★ ★ ★ ★
Updating:	Occasionally	Content:	★ ★ ★ ★
Navigation:	★ ★ ★ ★ ★	Speed:	★ ★ ★ ★ ★

UK

Originally these pages were set up to support BBC2's Bloodties programme, but have been expanded into a very creditable family history section. It offers one of the best introductions to the whole business of doing UK-based family history research on the web. Note that the double chevron at the bottom right of each page is your link to the next page, while the black button in the centre returns you to the index.

SPECIAL FEATURES

Family History If you're fairly new to genealogy, start with this excellent introduction. It will guide you through using family resources, searching public records, consulting censuses and other materials.

Advanced Genealogy This excellent eight-part guide by Else Churchill is very useful when you've outgrown the basic information sources and are ready to tackle wills, directories, poor law records, court records, migration records and other less obvious sources.

Heraldry/Coats of Arms are two similarly clear explanatory pages.

History is interesting but probably only of use if it happens to address a topic you are researching, because it is focused on the BBC's own recent programmes rather than being a directory of history resources in general.

Links provides good basic lists of all the major websites (detailed elsewhere in this book), helpfully divided by country: England and Wales first, then Scotland, then Northern Ireland and the Republic of Ireland.

Victorian Studio Photographs gives a comprehensive guide to the family history clues that can be gained from family photos.

Mugshots is a gallery of rather poignant Victorian photos from the Birmingham Police Museum archive. If you are lucky (or unlucky?) you may find one of your ancestors here.

Afro-Caribbean Family History provides a very welcome overview of the sources available and the particular challenges of tracing afro-caribbean ancestors.

Top Tips by Kathy Chater could save you some time and effort in your researches.

Local History gives advice about researching the history of your home or town.

Oral History introduces the wealth of material in the BBC archives.

Message Boards are well used, but are perhaps too general and too populated with newbies to be of much use. For more knowledgeable forums you're probably best to graduate to the subject-specific forums hosted by RootsWeb (see p.39)

What a wonderful starting point. It deserves exploration by any new-to-genealogy researcher and increasingly has something to offer the more experienced.

www.genuki.org.uk

GENUKI: The UK & Ireland Genealogical Information Service

Overall rating: ★ ★ ★ ★

Classification:	General	Readability:	★ ★ ★ ★ ★
Updating:	Regularly	Content:	★ ★ ★ ★
Navigation:	★ ★ ★ ★ ★	Speed:	★ ★ ★ ★ ★

UK

Without question the most important website of general use to UK researchers, and one you will return to again and again, whatever your level of expertise, GENUKI is a 'virtual reference library' of genealogical data. It is important to understand that this is mainly a library of primary source material, drawn from historical documentation, and is not secondary (or tertiary – see Introduction) material such as GEDCOM files assembled by individuals. To get an immediate idea of its massive scope, click on the logo in the central box. It hosts an enormous number of pages on the GENUKI server and provides links to many more, elsewhere.

SPECIAL FEATURES

Guidance for First-Time Users is the best place to start. Under the heading 'How this information server is organised', there is a link to 'standards observed by each of the providers', and it is these that earn GENUKI its high reliability rating. Further down the page is Published Papers about this Server which, should demonstrate why this website is held in such high regard worldwide.

Getting Started in Genealogy is located in the yellow boxes in the middle of the page, and comprises an article and bibliography to inform those researching family history for the first time. Read this before asking obvious questions on message boards – nothing is more likely to alienate those who can help, if you clearly haven't tried to help yourself.

FAQs is exceptionally useful, and possibly a more immediately informative place to start exploring the site than through Contents at top right of the homepage, which leads mainly to a list of British and Irish counties.

World Genealogy, Newsgroups and Bulletin Boards leads you to a number of newsgroups devoted to various topics and regions, worldwide. This is where internet genealogy comes into its own, harnessing the knowledge, experience and problem-solving abilities of an international community.

Contents and Search (top right of page), however, has vital information slightly 'buried' in the first few lines. First, at the bottom of the introductory paragraph, there is a link to the GENUKI Search Engine, which will search all GENUKI pages. And immediately below that is an apparent repeat of GENUKI Contents, which does admittedly say 'not to be overlooked'. True indeed, as you will see when you look at it. This will give you a sense of the full scope of this site. Among the very useful pages you will find are listings by county, indexes of surname lists and look-up exchanges, where volunteers with access to original documents or directories willl perform free searches on your behalf.

GENEVA is the list of forthcoming or, as they put it with a gentle nod to American users, 'upcoming' events which appears in the last of the yellow boxes.

Recent Changes to these Pages is most easily consulted by scrolling down, rather than using the date boxes.

The most complete, most user-friendly general site for British users. It is impossible here to convey the diversity of the information this site presents to you, so spend plenty of time exploring. If you can't find anything to help you here, you're in trouble indeed.

www.rootsweb.com
RootsWeb.com

Overall rating: ★ ★ ★ ★ ★			
Classification:	General	Readability:	★ ★ ★ ★
Updating:	Regularly	Content:	★ ★ ★ ★ ★
Navigation:	★ ★ ★ ★	Speed:	★ ★ ★ ★

US

This is the internet's oldest and largest free genealogy site, though ironically its excellent works are supported by Ancestry.com, the commercial behemoth that attracts much negative comment from the online community. The homepage offers two search facilities, where you can search either RootsWeb or Ancestry.com for names. Below this, however, is probably the best place to start. Here there are about 60 links under headings **Getting Started, Search Engines and Databases, Family Trees, Mailing Lists, Message Boards, Research Templates, Web Sites, Other Tools and Resources, Hosted Volunteer Projects, Help** (including Frequently Asked Questions), **Buy or Sell,** and **Contributing to Rootsweb.**

SPECIAL FEATURES

Hosted Volunteer Genealogy Projects is one of the most useful sections, and most of these have matured in the last two years to the extent that they are reviewed elsewhere; such as FreeBMD (see p.55), FreeReg (p.59) and Random Acts of Genealogical Kindness (p.67).

Mailing Lists and Message Boards It is almost inevitable that you will end up subscribing here at some point. To find out why, see pp. 38-40.

The commitment of RootsWeb to a completely free service deserves wholehearted support, and the constantly improving quality of the resources, as well as the increasingly international nature (as opposed to mainly American) of the information it contains, will make this a favourite.

www.englishorigins.com
English Origins

Overall rating: ★ ★ ★ ★			
Classification: Records		**Readability:**	★ ★ ★ ★
Updating:	Regularly	**Content:**	★ ★ ★ ★ ★
Navigation:	★ ★ ★ ★	**Speed:**	★ ★ ★ ★ ★

UK R

It is the way of the future: fully indexed and searchable online transcriptions giving you fast access to primary records. But at a price, albeit a reasonable one. After its successful collaboration with the Scottish PRO to put national records online at Scots Origins (see p.85), Origins.net has teamed up with the Society of Genealogists to put some of its precious indexes online, as well as developing their own indexes of records from other sources for the English site. The site is clean, fast and efficient .

SPECIAL FEATURES

Free Surname Search gives you a sense of what records are held relating to your surname (though of course, it may be that none of them are your ancestors) enabling you to decide whether to subscribe. £6 gives you up to 48 hours to complete your research, allowing you to download up to 150 records. Members of the SoG have quarterly free access as a perk of membership.

The Databases are currently the Marriage Licence Allegations Index 1694-1850, Boyd's Marriage Index 1538-1840, London Apprenticeship Abstracts (1442-1850), Bank of England Will Extracts Index 1717-1845, Prerogative Court of Canterbury Wills Index 1750-1800, Archdeaconry Court of London Wills Index 1700-1807, and London Consistory Court Depositions Index 1700-1713. In each case the completeness of the coverage varies by county, so do check the information on each of the datasets first. New datasets are in preparation.

Help and Tips It is a strong-willed person who will bother to read this section before typing the surnames of those elusive ancestors into the search box, but if you do you will be rewarded with good searching tips and clear instructions about how to access the database. Ordering Hard Copies explains that for £10 each you can order hard copies of records from the Marriage Licence Allegations and the Bank of England Will Extracts. These will then be mailed to you by the SoG.

What's New leads you back to the Origins.net site from which you can access the How to Trace Your Family History, a good introduction for beginners, or transfer to Scots Origins (one look at which will make Sassenachs mad with jealousy at the foresight of the Scottish government in putting its records online).

Discussion Group This forum is hosted on Yahoo Groups, with the aim for users of mutual help in their searches and to find common ancestors, though this may be better achieved on more focused groups elsewhere.

Resources is where to find onward links divided under Books, Discussion Groups & Mailing Lists, Professional Researchers, Source Records Archives, Websites and Family History Articles.

When you consider the costs of travelling to records centres, this seems a small price to pay for convenience of researching from home on an easy-to-use site.

www.genealogy.com

Genealogy.com

Overall rating: ★ ★ ★ ★			
Classification: General		**Readability:**	★ ★ ★
Updating: Regularly		**Content:**	★ ★ ★
Navigation: ★ ★ ★ ★		**Speed:**	★ ★ ★ ★

US R 🔒

The homepage for this large well-known site is far less cluttered than it was, though advertisements remain intrusive. It is well organised, however, particularly as the card-file tabs along the top of the page reappear on every page you subsequently open, so moving between sections is easy and rapid. The site is now owned by American media group A&E and has a much more commercial feel, professional but twee. They also own the popular Family Tree Maker software package (see p.158), which is promoted at every opportunity on the site.

SPECIAL FEATURES

Search Use the Family Finder to search for ancestors across the whole of the internet. This allows you to search for names with birth and death dates, and locations, to narrow it down. Site Search helps you to find features at Genealogy.com.

Learning Center is aimed at new users, with 'How to...' articles on building up, recording and sharing a personal family history. There are online courses to follow on further topics such as creating an online homepage at genealogy.com. The Glossary takes you straight to a massive dictionary of archaic and legal terms, as well as commonly used abbreviations. The Helpful Websites section claims to contain over 50,000 links, classified in a way that requires you to dig through several levels to find what you need.

Strangely only one obscure site is listed for the United Kingdom, but nine for Albania.

MyGenealogy.com This is where you can create and store an online tree using the Web Edition of Family Tree Maker. Your data will then be compared to other sources to find matches. You can save, print or download your tree or publish it as a homepage, or contribute to the World Family Tree. As you have to be online to work on your tree, this is probably only a viable option for people with unlimited surfing packages. My Online Data Library allows you to scan both free-to-access sources and some for which you pay. These include World Family Tree (submitted by other users), 1900 US census, and International and Passenger Records, but you need to subscribe for access to these ($79.99 per year, $14.99 per month, or free with software packages.) These datasources are more useful for tracing US connections than British ancestors, and you are strongly advised to take the option to 'Get more details about this data' before subscribing or purchasing. For example, UK 1851 census records are offered without making it clear that this is the 2% sample with some additions rather than the whole thing.

Community offers, among other things, The Virtual Cemetery, where you can contribute an electronic memorial, adding photographs if you wish, or view an existing tombstone – an idea that may become very popular. The GenForum message boards and family home pages make up the rest.

Shop takes you to the Genealogy Store where you can buy various Family Tree Maker packages, and subscriptions to the data collections. Book and videos are also offered.

This is a big, big site with plenty of useful material to offer, which makes it a good place to start if you are going to tackle American sites at all. The online Glossary is particularly handy.

Links

Many of the sites listed under other headings in the book will provide useful links to other sources, and these will generally be noted in the individual reviews. These though are excellent starting points, sites whose principal interest for users in their onward links.

www.cyndislist.com			
Cyndi's List of Genealogy Sites on the Internet			
Overall rating: ★ ★ ★ ★ ★			
Classification:	General	Readability:	★ ★ ★ ★ ★
Updating:	Regularly	Content:	★ ★ ★ ★
Navigation:	★ ★ ★ ★	Speed:	★ ★ ★ ★ ★
US			

Cyndi's List has become a genealogical institution. This vast, extraordinary website is run by the amazing Cyndi Howells, genealogy obsessive and family-loving, all-American mom. Predominantly purple in colour, with shadowy red oak leaves scattered around each page, it's friendly, chatty and personal in what most UK users will think a very American style. BUT, listing as it does every genealogy website she knows, it's an absolute mine of information. At the time of writing Cyndi is receiving hundreds of emails every day. She has posted over 180,000 sites and has welcomed over 30-million visitors.

Husband Mark has put together what UK users may well find is one of the most useful parts of the site. 'Researching Ancestors from the United Kingdom' (his picture's available under 'About Mark Howells' at the end of the article) is a seven-page run-down of how to get going, which you may find worthwhile to print off. To find this, go to FAQs, then Personal Questions (bottom of page), then Mark and Cyndi's Family Tree, then Mark's Research, Including the UK & Ireland, and, finally, to the required article.

Overall, the site would have merited five stars in every category, except that Cyndi herself gives several very sensible warnings about trusting the information supplied, as it is simply not possible for her to check the reliability of everything submitted.

SPECIAL FEATURES

Cyndi's List Category Indexes & Search Engine offers her entire list of websites sorted in a number of different ways, such as in a 'No-Frills' form, by alphabetical order or by topics, a useful first method of sifting through this vast resource.

Scroll down the homepage for the **Main Index,** or choose to search in one the ways offered by the list on the top-right-hand of the home page:

Topical Index is perhaps the simplest way to get on top of the sheer number of sites listed, breaking them down into the following useful categories, each of which is further subdivided:

- Localities (it is worth checking out both United Kingdom and the separate countries. For example, England will also lead you to a very useful list of county-specific links).

- Ethnic Groups and People

- Immigration, Emigration and Migration

- Religions

- Records

- Research Tools and Reference Materials

- Help from Others

- Marketplace

- History

- Military

- Computers and the internet

- Miscellaneous

Other ways of viewing the links are:

Alphabetical Index, 'No Frills' index which omits update dates, descriptions or cross-referencing between categories.

Text Only Index is the quickest to load and navigate, and Search allows you do that if you prefer.

Browse the New Links details all the new sites submitted in the last three months.

CyndisList Mailing List gives details of how to become a subscriber, while How to Submit a New Link to Cyndi's List is self-explanatory.

Internet Stuff You Need to Know gives some very worthwhile warnings about such annoyances as spam, chain-letters, hoaxes and computer viruses, as well as helpful tips on terminology, netiquette, search engines and privacy issues.

Cyndi's Genealogy Home Page Construction Kit is just what it says: a guide to creating your own family tree homepage, with lists of free or reasonably priced page-hosting services, to putting your details into a GEDCOM format, designing a website either yourself or using a professional, and such important things as how to cope with updating and where to advertise your website.

The links from this site are numerous. The best starting point is Frequently Asked Questions. Under 'Why do you do all this?', Cyndi answers, 'because I have fun', and also explains what Cyndi's List is: '... the internet is like a library with its books strewn all over the floor. I guess I'd like my list to be the card catalog for the genealogy section of that library.'

www.tcwaters.free-online.co.uk/
Ibertek

Overall rating: ★ ★ ★ ★			
Classification:	General	**Readability:**	★ ★ ★ ★ ★
Updating:	Regularly	**Content:**	★ ★ ★ ★
Navigation:	★ ★ ★ ★	**Speed:**	★ ★ ★ ★ ★

UK

This almost bafflingly large gateway website does everything any of the similar American sites do, with the great advantage that it is actually UK-based – in North Yorkshire. It is maintained by T.C. Waters, publishers and distributors of computer, history and education products. in what may seem a rather confusing presentation, simply move your cursor over each page to find the links, and don't ignore the 'next' button.

SPECIAL FEATURES

Enter Click the rose-window button at the bottom of the homepage to start exploring. The green buttons give access to a number of general categories, of which Genealogy Links 1 and 2 will be your best starting point. From the first of these a multitude of further links is given, carefully and logically sorted in a subject index that includes International Genealogy, Maritime Records, Maps & Topography, and so on. Within each of these categories another further list of links is given.

Here, you can find out about everything from deciphering Egyptian hieroglyphics to getting the letters of your own name put into as many anagrams as is humanly possible. Amazing!

Both fun and serious, this site will seek out almost any genealogical resource. Even if you don't find what you want, serendipity will lead you down some extraordinary avenues.

www.joesgenealogy.com
Joe's Genealogy 2000

Overall rating: ★ ★ ★ ★			
Classification:	General	**Readability:**	★ ★ ★ ★
Updating:	Occasionally	**Content:**	★ ★ ★
Navigation:	★ ★ ★ ★	**Speed:**	★ ★ ★ ★

UK

http://www.oplin.lib.oh.us
Ohio Public Library Information Network

Overall rating: ★ ★ ★ ★			
Classification:	General	**Readability:**	★ ★ ★ ★
Updating:	Rarely	**Content:**	★ ★ ★
Navigation:	★ ★ ★	**Speed:**	★ ★

US

Below the grey box that runs right across the homepage is a list of all the things Joe's website purveys, from his Hints for Beginners to See Where Joe is Doing a Talk, and a list of Joe's Guides or Other Shareware Genealogy Software.

SPECIAL FEATURES

Click on the blue 'Go' buttons to open any of the pages.

What's New! At the time of testing, this section offered the opportunity to check out the World's Top 100 Genealogy Sites, which was interesting to do, even though they proved to be predominantly American.

Surf Through Many Genealogy Related Web Sites Listed links to a lengthy and most useful list, though several of those tested proved unavailable. This, of course, is one of the hazards of doing research on the internet. When websites close down or are discontinued for whatever reason, usually nobody remembers to inform the search engines and portals where they have been listed.

The penultimate button allows you to sign up to receive Joe's free newsletters by email.

This is certainly worth exploring in some detail, partly for the helpful basic information logged here, and partly for the vast range of onward links.

This website, and the next one, are two good places to check what is new in the Genealogy world. The American websites are typically very quick to upload new information. Click on Genealogy in the left margin as your starting point.

http://www.genhomepage.com
The Genealogy Homepage

Overall rating: ★ ★ ★			
Classification:	General	**Readability:**	★ ★ ★
Updating:	Rarely	**Content:**	★ ★ ★
Navigation:	★ ★ ★	**Speed:**	★ ★

US

Like the previous site, this is another very up-to-date source of information, as you will see from the What's New and What's Really New links.

LDS and the IGI

The works and websites produced by the Church of Jesus Christ of the Latter Day Saints (LDS for short) deserve a section all of their own, even though they will be cross-referenced continually througout this book.

www.familysearch.com			
FamilySearch Internet Genealogy Service			
Overall rating: ★ ★ ★ ★			
Classification:	General	**Readability:**	★ ★ ★ ★
Updating:	Regularly	**Content:**	★ ★ ★ ★
Navigation:	★ ★ ★ ★ ★	**Speed:**	★ ★ ★ ★
US			

Here you will find the famous IGI (International Genealogical Index), more popularly known as the Mormon Index, created by the members of the Church of Jesus Christ of Latter-Day Saints, whose headquarters are in Salt Lake City, Utah. On your first visit it might be worth consulting About the Church of Jesus Christ of Latter-Day Saints (left-hand column) just to understand what this is all about. In no doubt simplified terms, members of the Church believe that they can baptise ancestors, posthumously, into the Mormon faith, so to find those ancestors they are compiling a massive database of family history records. Some record holders have refused access, and those records have not been transcribed. The great majority, however, have been amenable and the result is the most massive, free, online genealogical database in the world.

SPECIAL FEATURES

The main sections of the site are indicated in tabs across the top of the page.

Home provides access to News, FAQs (now called Family Search Questions), and Order/Download products. The latter includes free genealogy software, such as the Personal Ancestral File (PAF) in various versions, and other useful documents.

Search offers you an immediate opportunity to start looking for your ancestors. Provided you know the name(s) you are looking for, you don't need to worry about filling in further details of dates and events unless you are very certain of them, otherwise you may get less information rather than more.

As usual, required fields to fill in are indicated by asterisks. Tips for searching are offered from a link in purple letters just above the search boxes, and are well worth reading.

There are several different databases to search from: **All Resources**; **Ancestral File** (which combines all submissions on each individual); **IGI** (the most authoritative and useful for UK researchers); **Pedigree Resource Files**, which have been submitted by individual researches and so are of variable accuracy; **US Social Security Death Index; Vital Records** (currently only covers Mexican and Scandinavian records online through there is a separate CD with British records); and **Search Family History Websites.**

Also within the Search section you'll find the **Research Guidance.** Start by specifying the country you need to research, then the type of event (birth, death or marriage) and the approximate timeframe, and you'll be presented with concise run-downs of the relevant types of records available to help your research and details of where to consult them. It is true to say that the lists that then appear need to be approached with a good deal of selectivity.

Small, local family history societies are mixed up with major record-holding bodies, in no logical order, and there are some out-of-date inaccuracies. As a route to the records of other countries, however, this still has to be considered a very valuable starting point.

Research Helps is a library of documents, most available as PDF files, on subjects such as how to use Church records. You can search by place, title, subject or document type. Although rather tucked away this is well worth browsing.

Web Sites can be searched or browsed by category.

Share leads you to **Collaboration Email Lists, Add a Web Site to Family Search** and **Share My Genealogy.** All require registration to participate but, once you have your own records in order, you may well feel it worthwhile to do so, more so if you have US relatives.

LIBRARY is mostly of interest if you are planning to visit their vast library in Salt Lake City, but under **Family History Centres** you can search for the closest centre to you, and they are scattered all over the world. Each of these has considerable holdings in its own right and can help you source other items from the main library. **Family History Library Catalog** allows you to search the vast genealogical holdings. Items on microfilm or fiche can be ordered for viewing at your local Family History Centres. In general it is not possible to request books on loan, but it is sometimes possible to arrange for the originals to be microfilmed, though you may need to wait for several months.

This is the real thing, the most indispensable online resource on the entire web. And it grows more and more impressive daily (look at What's New in Site Map in the blue toolbar at the top of the page).

Latter-day Saints Online
http://lds.org.uk
This will send you to the Latter Day Saints' British website. Under Family History you'll find a link to a list of the UK Family History Centres that includes phone numbers. There is also a link to the Church's own very useful software and CD-roms, including the 1881 Census, and the British Isles Vital Records Index (BVRI), which acts as a supplement to the IGI. This is found under Church Produced Software.

Steve's Quick Guide to the www.familysearch.org website
http://members.lycos.co.uk/familyhistory2/fs.htm
If you are at all confused about how to use the IGI, this long one-page tutorial is invaluable, especially the explanation of batch numbers.

International Genealogical Index (IGI) Batch Numbers
http://www.genuki.org.uk/big/FindingBatchNos.html
Genuki's explanation of batch numbers.

The LDS FamilySearch Website: Using the Batch Numbers
http://globalgazette.net/gazfd/gazfd36.htm
Gives an in-depth guide to the batch number system and how to use it. Substitute 40 for 36 in this URL to read an article on using batch numbers to obtain original records.

Instructions for using IGI Batch Numbers
www.rootsweb.com/~engken/batchnumbers.txt
Short, step-by-step instructions are followed by an alphabetical listing of towns in Kent with their batch numbers.

Mailing lists, message boards and newsgroups

The terminology can be confusing, and names are often used interchangeably, but mailing lists, message boards, newsgroups and forums all allow you to interact through your computer with other people who share the same interests as you.

Working on the principle that a problem shared is a problem halved, if not solved, you can draw on the experience of people with varying levels of expertise and specialist knowledge who may be able to suggest new ways through a knotty problem. These media also act as grapevines where you will hear about new sites, new products, and which ones to avoid.

MAILING LISTS

When you subscribe to a mailing list, or email list, you start to receive copies of all the messages posted to the list by other members, delivered to you by email. Usually you have a choice of subscribing either in list mode, where each message is sent to you separately as soon as it is received, or has been approved by the listowner, or in digest mode, where you receive several messages bundled in a single email.

For very active lists the amount of email you receive can be daunting until you learn that you don't have to read every single one. You will become adept at skimming subject lines, or the body of the email to search for the particular threads (correspondence on a particular subject) that interest you. But don't be too selective: there are many enormously knowledgeable people on these lists and there is much that can be learnt from their answers to other people's queries, even if they do not seem directly relevant to your own research.

Be aware that most lists are very well established, and although newcomers are generally welcomed and indulged, it is courteous to get a feel for the list and types of topics that come up before launching in. Make sure you have read the chapters for 'newbies' on GENUKI (see p.29) or some other introductory material. If the list has an FAQ section or message boards ('mailing list gateways') or archives, read them first, to ensure that what you're asking hasn't been asked a thousand times before. Or start off gently with a list such as Gen-Newbie@rootsweb.com, for those who are new to both internet and genealogy.

Don't expect other people to do your research for you. Just putting down some names and dates and asking for any information will not get you many responses (at least not polite ones!). But people do go out of the way to help and look-up requests are generally fulfilled if they are reasonable. Try to make your request as specific as possible, and provide as much relevant detail as you can.

MESSAGE BOARDS

Also known as forums, or discussion groups, message boards have much the same function as mailing lists, but instead of posts (messages) being emailed to you, they are collected on a website to be viewed online. This is usually a slower way of reading messages than mailing lists or newsgroups.

There are mailing lists and message boards for almost every aspect of genealogy and family history you can think of, with the biggest selection being hosted by RootsWeb (see below), and many sites will invite you to join their mailing list. This should not be confused with subscribing to a newsletter, which is a one-way communication rather than interactive.

NEWSGROUPS

Newsgroups were the original mainstay of the wired communities, but have largely been superseded by mailing lists as a more convenient way of accessing information. To join a newsgroup you have to install special newsreading software and your ISP has to support the particular news server that hosts the group you want to join. Most recent versions of web browsers such as Netscape Navigator or Internet Explorer will allow you to access your ISP's news server.

Messages are posted straight to, and downloaded from, these news servers rather than being distributed by email. You need to download the list of all the newsgroups that your ISP permits access to. The lists are generally vast, so this can take some time. You can then select which groups to participate in. Most of the genealogy groups have names that take the form soc.genealogy.nameofgroup, such as soc.genealogy.britain, soc.genealogy.surrnames, or soc.genealogy.surnames.britain. For a more convenient way of accessing newsgroups, see groups.google.com below.

MAILING LIST SITES

www.familychronicle.com/maillist.html
A superbly detailed article by Mark Howells, providing everything you ever need to know about mailing lists. An indispensable starting point.

http://lists.rootsweb.com
This is the main index to the 26,000 plus mailing lists hosted by RootsWeb. These are grouped by Surnames A-Z, USA states, International countries A-Z (note that there are entries for United Kingdom and the individual countries, England Scotland, Wales and Ireland), and other topics.

http://archiver.rootsweb.com
Here you can gain access to the archived messages from any of the RootsWeb mailing lists. It helps if you know which mailing list you want, otherwise you have to browse through an alphabetical listing of many thousands of groups. Messages are archived by threads, so you can see all the replies to an original post in the order they were posted, as though following a conversation.

www.genuki.org.uk/indexes/MailingLists.html
GENUKI has collected together the mailing lists relevant to those with research interests in specific areas of the British Isles, and cross references them with the descriptions from John Fuller's list.

MESSAGE BOARDS

http://boards.rootsweb.com
This gateway to the RootsWeb message boards is organised in the same way as the mailing lists index: by Surnames, Localities and Topics, or you can search all the messages posted on all the boards for mention of any particular names words or phrases, or search to find a board dedicated to the name or topic you are interested in.

www.rootsweb.com/~jfuller/gen_mail_country-link-gen.html
Even when you think you have explored all Rootsweb's mailing list avenues, do still have a look at this GB-specific selection.

NEWSGROUPS

http://homepages.rootsweb.com/~socgen/Britain.htm

This page provides plenty of information about newsgroups in general, and you can click through on the names of individual groups to find the group's charter (rules of engagement), rationale, FAQs and any associated mailing list, web pages or archives.

http://groups.google.com

Google took over the role of Deja.com, which archived newsgroups and gave web access via an ordinary browser to newsgroups, which is useful if your ISP does not have a news server, or you do not use a browser that includes news server reader software. The majority of genealogy groups are in the soc section. Take time to read the Google Groups Help (to the side of the search box) before taking the plunge.

FORUMS, DISCUSSION GROUPS AND COMMUNITIES

http://Genforum.genealogy.com

GenForum hosts over 20,000 surname forums, as well as topic- and country-specific forums.

http://smartgroups.com
http://uk.groups.yahoo.com

Each of these sites allows you to join or set up your own online community, and they have thriving genealogy groups.

Genealogical Societies

www.ffhs.org.uk			
Federation of Family History Societies			
Overall rating: ★ ★ ★ ★			
Classification:	General	Readability:	★ ★ ★ ★ ★
Updating:	Regularly	Content:	★ ★ ★ ★
Navigation:	★ ★ ★ ★ ★	Speed:	★ ★ ★ ★
UK			

Formed in 1974, the Federation now has a membership of over 220 societies, some national, some regional, and some that represent only one-name studies. Their twice-yearly journal is Family History News and Digest, but they also publish a number of books and information leaflets. All member societies receive a copy of the Handbook, in which each of them automatically receives a listing.

SPECIAL FEATURES

ABC of FFHS gives you a rundown of the society's activities and organisation.

Help with Research is the most rewarding section. It leads to First Steps, where you will find Your Questions, always a good route to discovering what any particular organisation does. Research Services explains that many societies do not have the resources to cope with the vast number of queries that are put to them, and outlines the ways in which you, as a person requesting information, can help by making your enquiry as clear as possible. Given that their work is normally done free of charge, it is particularly important that you observe these recommendations, and are not too impatient about getting immediate answers.

The Strays Clearing House and the National Strays Index form a vital resource for those seeking ancestors who are difficult to track because they are recorded as being 'from' or connected with somewhere other than the area in which they normally lived. As the explanatory notes say, these records are 'greatly under-used'. Sometimes they contain the vital clue that de-bugs a long-standing problem. They can't be consulted online, but your nearest FHS will have them on microfiche, or you can order them from the Federation – instructions are provided at the bottom of the page.

Adopted Persons is self-explanatory, and the Federation may be able to help when other searches have failed.

Record Offices offers excellent advice on how to prepare for a visit to your County Record Office.

Soldier Ancestors is a very clear guide to the whereabouts and contents of military records.

Federation Projects Among projects currently being supported are the National Burials Index (NBI), National Inventory of War Memorials and continuing work on the indexing of census returns and other records. The Federation also runs courses and conferences, and represents the interests of its membership at national level.

Conferences and Fairs gives details of the Federation's own half-yearly conferences (very well in advance) and a link through the GENEVA project to many others.

Contacting our Members puts you in touch with regional societies, one-name studies and other specialist societies such as Railway Ancestors and the Catholic FHS.

Publications takes you to a separate site of Family History Books, where you can purchase publications by the various societies and other genealogical books on a secure server.

A vital website for any family history enthusiast, which should persuade you of the value of joining your local FHS.

www.sog.org.uk
The Society of Genealogists

Overall rating: ★ ★ ★ ★ ★			
Classification: General		**Readability:**	★ ★ ★ ★ ★
Updating: Regularly		**Content:**	★ ★ ★ ★ ★
Navigation: ★ ★ ★ ★		**Speed:**	★ ★ ★ ★ ★

UK

The Society of Genealogists is a charity whose object is to support, both by research facilities and personal guidance, those interested in tracing their family history. All links are exceptionally clear and, without images, speed is excellent. When the homepage appears it may look complete, but, in fact, you need to scroll down to see it all.

SPECIAL FEATURES

Information, which is the best introduction for newcomers, is rather oddly half-way down the page. It tells how to contact the society and opening hours. Membership tells you about subscription rates, and the committe procedure to approve membership. You can't sign up online but, if you've been convinced of the value of joining, you can download an application form. Information Leaflets should not be missed. Here you can read about topics such as Note Taking and Keeping for Genealogists, the Right to Arms, and a Practical Guide to Employing a Professional Researcher.

Library is a massive resource, with over 9,000 transcriptions of Parish Registers, County Records, Census material, Poll Books and Directories. It also contains much material on the professions, the services, the peerage, religious denominations, schools and universities – an absolutely essential starting point. Particularly useful is the 'Before Coming to the Library' advice, which suggests preparatory work you should do to make your visit more productive.

Money from the Heritage Lottery Fund has been used to computerise the catalogue of their holdings, but this is unfortunately not available online. However, clicking on Parish Register Copies, found under Library Holdings, will tell you county by county, and then by place name exactly, which registers and for what years are in the collection. Some may even be borrowed by members.

Bookshop With over 6000 items in stock, including books, maps, microfiche, software, and data CDs, the SoG Bookshop claims to be the largest of its kind in the UK. Online ordering is secure, but browsing is not easy, and the navigation icons are by no means self evident. If you want to search, click on the row of question marks.

Lectures & FH Fairs & other Events gives information about the Society's lectures and courses, most of which are held at their own premises in London, with some further afield, as well as visits to such museums and archives.

Projects includes details of recent and ongoing ambitious projects undertaken by volunteers, such as producing surname indexes of marriage licences from various major sources. The first of these are already available in book and microfiche form, and online through Origins (see below).

Society Data Online gives details of mailing lists, hosted by RootsWeb, and other online material currently available. It would be good to see more in this section, though in this section you'll find the link to **English Origins,** which is is the main change since the last edition of this guide. Membership of the SoG allows a certain amount of free access each quarter to the SoG's records held on Origins.net.

The Society On-line offers **Genealogists' Magazine** and **Computers in Genealogy,** the Society's own publications, with good details of the contents of both current and past issues. Articles and reviews that are over a year old can be read online.

General is the last section in the menu but is worth looking at earlier as it contains a Web Site Map which is the best way of gaining an overview of the site, the last item in which is, what should be, the useful 'What's New'; except that in early September 2003 only things that were new in 2001 were listed! Try **Latest News** from the homepage instead.

Links is actually a way in to a very useful page headed 'Essential websites'. Bookmarking this as a first-stop entry point might be a very natty, shortcut way of accessing many other highly useful organisations, without the need to list them all individually. Have a look and see what you think.

A brilliantly simple, rapid site for finding out what material the Society owns, where to find it and what other organisations to approach.

www.familyhistoryonline.net		
Family History Online		
Overall rating: ★ ★ ★		
Classification: General	**Readability:**	★ ★ ★
Updating: Regularly	**Content:**	★ ★ ★
Navigation: ★ ★ ★	**Speed:**	★ ★ ★
UK		

This is a very new, pay-per-view service introduced by the Federation of Family History Societies. It claims to hold well over 8 million searchable records and you can buy vouchers from £5 upwards, which are valid for six months. So far, it covers only England and Wales and, as yet, nowhere near all counties – but this is a resource to watch

Official records

In a sense this is where your real research will probably start: the task of gathering civil registration certificates and delving into public records will make you feel like a real researcher.

www.familyrecords.gov.uk			
Family Records Centre			
Overall rating: ★ ★ ★ ★ ★			
Classification: General		**Readability:**	★ ★ ★ ★ ★
Updating: Regularly		**Content:**	★ ★ ★ ★ ★
Navigation: ★ ★ ★ ★		**Speed:**	★ ★ ★ ★ ★
UK			

At the time of the first edition of this guide, it was just a link from the main PRO site (see p.44), but it has now graduated to a freestanding site, in recognition of its importance to the ever-increasing numbers of family researchers.

The Family Records Centre was established in 1997 by the PRO and the Office for National Statistics. **Topics** introduces the core of its collection, which is made up of indexes of births, marriages, deaths and adoptions, previously held at the General Register Office in St Catherine's House, London. These are the indexes you need to consult to find the references for ordering birth, marriage and death certificates. Guides to each of these can be read online and offer further internal links, so they are well worth investigating.

The FRC also holds census returns for England and Wales, previously held at the PRO itself in Chancery Lane.

Partners provides links to the main UK record offices, including A2A (Access to Archives), part of the PRO, as well as PRO of Northern Ireland, GRO, GRO Scotland, National Archives of Scotland, Llyfrgell Genedlaethol Cymru and the India Office Records, among others. You'll also find full details of the holdings, and information about how to get there and opening hours, essential if you're planning a visit.

SPECIAL FEATURES

The Family Record is the FRC's newsletter, available to be read online. Find it by typing the word 'magazine' in the search box on the homepage. In the resulting list it appears as Family Records Centre – Newsletter

Guides include Using the Internet for Family History, and Family History Guides. Find it by typing the word 'magazine' in the search box on the homepage. In the resulting list it appears as Family Records Centre Newsletter.

Incidentally, the PRO produces an extremely good and attractively illustrated booklet called 'The Family Records Centre Introduction to Family History'. Costing £3.99, it is available from the PRO itself (see p. 44).

THE vital resource, sooner or later, for all genealogists. A good deal of the same online information can be accessed through the Public Record Office website (see p.44), but this is a more direct route.

TIP If you can't get to the FRC in person to check their indexes try the Free BMD site (see p.56) or BDM EXchange (p.57), or you can consult microfiche versions of the indexes at many Family History Centres, run by the Latter Day Saints. To find your nearest centre, check http://www.lds.org.uk/genealogy/fhc/index.htm.

www.pro.gov.uk
The Public Record Office

Overall rating: ★ ★ ★ ★			
Classification: General		**Readability:**	★ ★ ★ ★ ★
Updating: Regularly		**Content:**	★ ★ ★ ★
Navigation: ★ ★ ★		**Speed:**	★ ★ ★ ★

UK 🔒

The PRO is one of the main repositories of the national archives. Its website claims 'it will inspire and inform you at all stages of your family history detective work'. The site's presentation and ambitions have improved immensely since the first edition of this book.

SPECIAL FEATURES

Start Your Research should be read before planning a visit. As well as explaining how the PRO works this section gives guidance for family historians, directs you to other government websites, and can help you find an independent researcher willing to conduct research on your behalf. Don't pass up the opportunity to link to the Family History Guides (which can be purchased online), the Family Records Leaflets (read online) and the Research Information Leaflets (download as PDF files) from the Family History section.

Catalogues gives you details of their holdings of over nine million records. PROCAT is the main database, but there are others including Hospital Records, Equity Pleadings, National Digital Archive of Datasets, A2A (the national Access to Archives project). You can also access an index of Research Information Leaflets through this link.

Online Records has seen the most progress since the last edition. The addition of a separate Census website (see p.60), the introduction of wills online (see p.63), an interactive introduction to Medieval Seals, and the cabinet documents from the Macmillan Administration are good examples of the PRO's commitment to deliver more of its holdings online, both in free and paid-for services. It is worth checking back regularly to see what has been added. Online payments are secure.

Quick Order When you've located the documents you need to consult in the catalogue you can order them online in advance so that you don't have to spend valuable research time waiting for the documents to be produced. If you can't attend the PRO in person you can pay £10 to have an estimate prepared for the cost of copying up to five documents.

Education As well as material aimed at school children, this section includes Pathways to the Past, an adult learning section presenting themed exhibitions on relevant historical subjects. All of the sections here are of interest to family historians, with Family History obviously being the most relevant.

Bookshop stocks the wide range of the PRO's very useful titles and provides simple and secure online ordering.

Events lists all the tours, conferences, workshops and special events organised by the PRO.

PRO News is a monthly, free e-newsletter, launched in February 2003, a good way of keeping up to date with new developments and forthcoming PRO events.

This is a slick site for a government body and the recent improvements show their commitment to the online delivery of primary records. Oddly, there is no apparent link to the PRO's new bi-monthly Ancestors *magazine, launched in April/May 2001. See p.162.*

www.tagish.co.uk/tagish/links/localgov.htm
Tagish – Local Government

★★★★★ UK

Tagish is a consultancy firm working with Local Government to help it get its information online. This page is a good starting point.

www.statistic.gov.uk
Office of National Statistics

★★★★ UK

Most of this very extensive website is dedicated to current statistics covering everything from the numbers of Optical Vouchers issued to patients needing spectacles to the fact that Jack and Chloe are currently the most popular baby names. Genealogists will be mainly interested in Birth, Marriage and Death Registration, in Related Websites.

This is where all the acronyms start to get confusing, even if you've managed to get your FRCs and your PROs sorted. The Office of National Statistics (ONS) oversees the General Register Office (GRO), which is responsible for indexing and issuing civil registration certificates (birth, deaths and marriages or BDMs). The GRO indexes are held at the FRC (with microfiche copies in some major libraries and at LDS FHCs), but unless you can attend the FRC in person, or employ a records agent, this is where apply to obtain certificates.

SPECIAL FEATURES

Certificates in England and Wales You can't order online, but you can download application forms in PDF format. This section also gives details about how to apply by post,

telephone or fax. It will also give you details of fees, which are more expensive than applying at the FRC, and even more if you don't have the exact GRO reference. There are links to the local registration offices that are online, as these will also supply, sometimes more cheaply, certificates of BDMs that were registered in their area, though the service varies considerably depending on the willingness of local staff.

Adoptions is another potentially useful part of the site, as it provides information on access to birth records, and the Adoption Contact Register is a confidential way for birth parents and other relatives to assure an adopted person that contact would be welcome.

This functional site, which also covers official UK statistics, has links to the Northern Ireland and Scottish equivalent sites, which are reviewed separately in Regional Resources.

www.ukonline.gov.uk
UK Online

★★★★ UK

The site's mission statement is to be 'the easy way to government information and services online'. As well as providing a gateway to all local and central government departments, it provides news of new services that are being put online to further the government's aim of making every part of its services accessible via the internet by 2005.

QuickFind gives an A-Z of Central Government and Local Government. The latter is of use to family historians trying to find county record offices, and local authorities and boroughs, which often have their own archives. You can use the search box to find the sites that you need. While here, you can find out how to report a crime online or consult

Libraries and archives

See also other libraries and archives reviewed in the Regional Resources chapter. The SoG has an extensive library for genealogists (see p.41), and the PRO (p.44) and PRONI (p.83) are respectively England and Northern Ireland's main repositories for public records .

www.bl.uk			
The British Library			
Overall rating: ★ ★ ★ ★ ★			
Classification:	Libraries	**Readability:**	★ ★ ★ ★ ★
Updating:	Regularly	**Content:**	★ ★ ★ ★ ★
Navigation:	★ ★ ★ ★	**Speed:**	★ ★ ★ ★
UK 🔒			

This simplest of URLs is the way into one of the richest websites available, as one might expect from the British Library.

The website is constantly being updated and is liberally adorned with photographs of the recently completed Library. If you hover your mouse over the top-of-page tabs, further drop-down menus will appear. Help if You Are ... is a good place to start exploring the site, with different introductions depending on what type of user you are. What's On, News and Contact Us are all offered from the main menu across the top of the page, but the following are likely to be of more use.

SPECIAL FEATURES

About Us On the Web describes the plans for making more collections and services available online, and is the quickest way of finding out about any new services added. **Gabriel,** found near the bottom of that page, is the 'Gateway to Europe's National Libraries', and is a resource of unimaginable scope. From here you can access major collaborative projects such as CERL (the Consortium of European Research Libraries) and the European Library.

Collections Provides an overview and links to the main collections, defined by region and type of collection (such as Maps, Manuscripts and Philatelic).

Catalogues This is another way of accessing the BLPC, from which you can search the main British Library catalogue of over 10 million items. Separate catalogues are available for newspapers, serials, manuscripts and sound archives.

Services brings up such delights as the Images Online, where several hours of browsing could be happily spent (it offers transparencies for hire) while those who have the right audio equipment could enjoy the Sound Archive, found under Collections. The Copy Services and Document Supply Services are an exciting development that permit you to search the Library's entire journal and conference collection, order directly over the web, and receive articles within two hours. The database starts from 1973, holds 10 million documents, and is expanding at the rate of 10 000 daily. Charges relate to the method of transmission, courier being the most expensive, first-class mail or 12-hour (as opposed to two hour) fax the cheapest.

What's On gives details of events and exhibitions, both current and future.

This is a huge site, impossible to describe in full detail here, but one well worth visiting, especially if you have the name of a book or author you need to track down, or if there is a matter of historical background you wish to research.

http://ihr.sas.ac.uk/gh

Guildhall Library (Corporation of London) Manuscripts Section

Overall rating: ★ ★ ★ ★

Classification:	Records	Readability:	★ ★ ★
Updating:	Regularly	Content:	★ ★ ★ ★
Navigation:	★ ★ ★	Speed:	★ ★ ★

UK

First click on General Guide to Collections, which explains (well down the page) the vital point to bear in mind, namely that the Manuscripts Section of the Guildhall Library is the local record office for the City of London (the geographical 'Square Mile') rather than the archives for the Corporation of London, which have their own Records Office (see below). The holdings date from the eleventh century, and consist mainly of records associated with London's local and taxation authorities, livery companies, courts of law, churches, charities, schools and businesses. Many of the collections, such as manorial documents, livery company and foreign register transcripts, justify the inclusion of the site here, rather than in the London Regional secion. Note that the four-star rating above relates not to the content of the collections, but the complications of finding one's way around this rather basic website.

SPECIAL FEATURES

Leaflet Guides to Records, also on the homepage, is another useful point from which to start. Each of the leaflets listed can be read in full online, and covers topics such as sources for tracing Apothecaries, Surgeons and Physicians, City Of London Livery Companies, Land Tax Assessments and registers of children at schools such as Christ's Hospital.

Other links go to Genealogical Sources at Guildhall Library, City of London Parish Records and Business Records at Guildhall Library, which date from the 15th century.

Livery Company Membership Guide points to a page at the bottom of which is a further link to the actual list of companies, including, alongside the familiar trades, such obscure terms as 'loriners' and 'poulters'.

London Metropolitan Archives contains, apparently, 31 miles of archives, and is the largest local authority record office in the UK.

Corporation of London Record Office (CLRO), also linked from this homepage is another major repository of documents relating to London.

If at any point you find ancestors in London, which is likely, you will probably need to consult this site, as well as the Corporation of London Records Office and the London Metropolitan Archives (reviewed on p.77). Few of the records can actually be read online, but at least you can establish which records might be of importance to you, and where they are. **Note**: *Re-building to improve storage facilities is being undertaken from February 2003 for at least five months, during which period many documents will not be available for consultation.*

www.hmc.gov.uk
Historical Manuscripts Commission

Overall rating: ★ ★ ★ ★			
Classification:	Historical	**Readability:**	★ ★ ★ ★ ★
Updating:	Occasionally	**Content:**	★ ★ ★ ★
Navigation:	★ ★ ★ ★	**Speed:**	★ ★ ★ ★

UK

There are two main collections to tempt the family historian here: the National Register of Archives (NRA) and ARCHON. Before rushing to explore these though, it is worth noting the following sections:

About HMC contain the What's New area, allowing you to check progress towards making more documents available online.

Manorial Documents Register Use this link to find out which documents are available online (Wales and parts of England) and where others can be located.

Advice offers limited information to researchers about accessing records, as well as advice to custodians about the care and preservation of documents.

Publications offers a vast number of reports and calendars, as well as books. It lists some that can be consulted online, but these are reports on archives and repositories rather than the actual documents they contain.

Archives in Focus is a very clearly presented section for use in education.

THE NATIONAL REGISTER OF ARCHIVES

The NRA was created by the Commission in 1945 to assemble and make available information about British history source material outside the main public records collections. The indexes of the collection are made available here online. It has nearly 250,000 lists of manuscript collections, ranging from those in private hands to special holdings in libraries, museums and local record offices, and can normally advise whether such papers are available for research.

The excellent online search facilities offer simple search by corporate name, personal name, family name and place name, or a more detailed search which varies with the particular index being searched.

Information Resources (currently 16) are lists of sources to consult on such topics as Business History, History of the Press, History of Education, Colonial History and so on. Testing by looking at 'Sources for Garden History', for instance, brought up an excellent list of relevant organisations to contact, with useful brief details of what the function of each is, as well as a brief bibliography.

ARCHON

The Archives On-line project is the information 'gateway' whereby archivists lodge the details of their holdings with the Commission. It provides an overview of which archival projects are planned, ongoing or completed, with links through to associated web pages. You can browse an alphabetical list of the projects by region or search by keyword, town or county. The database includes details of archives on individuals, families and organisations held in university libraries, which may not be indexed elsewhere online.

A clear, unfussy website probably of most use to those whose research is already fairly advanced and who are starting to explore somewhat more obscure resources.

www.a2a.pro.gov.uk
Access to Archives

★★★★★ UK

Part of the PRO's site described above (see p.44), the Access to Archives project provides access to catalogues and finding aids of English archives that have been submitted to the database. It has a highly efficient search facility. Ultimately you will probably be referred to the ARCHON database (see p.48), which is even more comprehensive in its coverage, but does not provide the same level of description of the sources. This is a web source of increasing value.

www.copac.ac.uk
COPAC

★★★★ UK

COPAC provides free access to the merged online catalogues of members of the Consortium of University Research Libraries, to which 23 major research institutions contribute. This does not therefore cover all British universities but Oxford, London, Cambridge, Edinburgh, and Trinity College, Dublin are all participants. Click on Libraries for a full list. User guides and FAQ page are worth consulting before launching into a search. A new user interface was in development at the time of review, so some of the details provided here may be subject to change. University libraries may not be obvious places to conduct genealogical research, but a search for parish registers produced over 3,500 items.

www.archiveshub.ac.uk
Archives Hub

★★★★ UK

This provides a national gateway to descriptions of archives in UK universities and colleges. There are over sixty repositories currently submitting collections (listed in About the Hub). Collections described range from the LSE's Poor Law collections to Dundee Health Board records and Family and Estate collections held at Bangor. You can browse the hub, or perform quick or advanced searches. Search results can be emailed to you, allowing you to store them for future reference.

www.archivesinfo.net/uksites.html
Archives Info

★★★ UK

A useful and straightforward way of finding achives with an internet presence, this site has a reasonably comprehensive set of links covering UK Archival Repositories on the Internet, Overseas Sites (arranged by country), Professional Associations, Current Projects and Archives Forum. Discussion Lists are aimed at professional archivists. Unfortunately the site has not been updated for some time, and so some of the links no longer work, but you can often work back to the homepage from a failed page request, and the brief descriptions of collections are useful. Of course there are now many more institutions online since these pages were created.

www.ask-a-librarian.org.uk
Ask a Librarian

★★★★★ UK

This relatively new service is a 24-hours-a-day, 365 days-a-year digital information facility. It is clear, easy to use and, at present, impressively rapid. You email your question and any one of some 70 participating libraries (nearly all, so far, in England) answers, also by email. It is not a family history searching service but it could, nevertheless, be a great help when all else fails.

Chapter 3

searching for names

By all means head immediately for a website that offers a name-search facility, type in the name you are interested in and hope for a result. Don't necessarily assume, however, that this is the best way of getting helpful information. One reason is that the majority of websites offering this facility are based in the United States, and although there are many families in this country with relatives across the Atlantic, there are still many more who have no American connections whatsoever. Nobody in the US is, therefore, likely to be researching those names, unless perhaps they are pursuing a lateral rather than a vertical (father-to-father) search. As the information contributed to name-search sites is mostly volunteered by individuals, you see the problem.

If you are serious about your family history you will need to do rather more digging, and the place to start is with civil registrations of birth, death and marriages, which with

some expenditure on certificates, should lead you back reasonably painlessly to somewhere between 1837 and 1875, providing lots of details and addresses along the way. In this chapter you will find the online sources that can help with this process.

Before civil registration began, parish registers provided the main records of an individual's life. The largest collection of these found online is in the IGI (see pp.36-7) but we have listed other sources to pursue. Wills, obituaries, passenger lists, land records, and of course the census provide further fruitful areas of search, with an increasing number of indexes and transcriptions, and even original records, available for online consultation.

Apart from sites dealing with these official records, there are myriad sources of names and possible connection on the net. The majority are derived from personal family trees, which are usually available online either as web pages or in GEDCOM (GEnealogical Data COMmunication) form.

Other people, instead of confining their search to their own family trees, compile one-name studies, which seek all occurrences, past and present, of a single surname, anywhere in the world. More often than not, they are most useful to the private researcher as a means of eliminating the inclusion of 'wrong' ancestors or branches of the family tree. You may, however, become fascinated by the wider aspects of the search, such as the geographical migration of the name or its persistence within certain professions, and wish to launch a one-name study of your own. If so, you can register with the Guild of One-Name Studies (GOONS, see p. 68), on the understanding that you will undertake to collect all references worldwide, not restricted by family or locality, and that you will personally deal with all reply-paid enquiries sent to you.

As a user of one-name studies websites, be warned that each site will only be as good as the person/people who contribute to it, so you may find that they are disorganised, that a lot of information is repeated rather than consolidated, and that response times are slow. Depending on the contributors, they may also, of course, be inaccurate. More usually, though, the sort of personalities attracted to such a Herculean task are meticulous, persistent and knowledgeable. Moreover, because one-name studies sites assemble information on a global scale, they are likely to become enormous, unless they are dealing with an unusual surname. Having offered those warnings, however, it may turn out that you find exactly the site, names and personal contacts you need and your researches will accordingly take a huge leap forward.

In addition to one-name sites, thousands of individuals have by now posted their own personal family trees on the web. They are also well worth exploring, especially those posted here in the UK, in case you find that someone else is researching the same branch of a family tree as you and is perhaps further along with their research. Allowing for the need to check the connections they have made (and good researchers will always document their sources), a lucky encounter of this sort could prove to be a shortcut to filling in a whole area of your own pedigree.

Alternatively, if you have already done lots of work yourself and have files of well-documented genealogical information about your own ancestors, you may want to post your own family tree on the web. You don't have to set up an independent website to do this. There are several website-hosting services that specialise in genealogy, not all requiring a subscription but usually needing to receive your file in GEDCOM form. There are websites on p.136 that tell you how to create your own GEDCOM.

Other sources of leads on names are the thousands of mailing lists, message boards or individual email contacts dedicated to single surnames, putting you in touch with people with shared interests, and with whom you can communicate, both asking and answering questions, sharing information and generally enjoying the whole field of ancestral research. There is more information about joining these groups on pp.38-40.

Finally, I have listed the sites where you can find genealogical angels: people with reference works such as trade directories, census indexes, and monumental records, who are willing to search their sources for your ancestors.

www.ancestry.com

Ancestry.com

Overall rating: ★ ★ ★			
Classification:	General	**Readability:**	★ ★
Updating:	Regularlyly	**Content:**	★ ★
Navigation:	★ ★	**Speed:**	★ ★

US £ 🔒

This site is reviewed first in this chapter, not because it should be your immediate destination, but because you are likely to be lured there by the search boxes promising access to millions of records that you will surely trip across very soon after starting to surf other genealogy sites. And secondly it appears here because the range of record types contained in Ancestry.com's databases mean that it covers probably every sub-section within this chapter.

A comment on the star rating of this site: Ancestry.com is the big daddy of commercial genealogy sites and if you want names, they are here by the million, culled from an enormous range of sources, including primary records and submitted data. The difficulty for a UK user is that unless you have American connections, you are unlikely to find much here of use, and a lot to distract (though see details of the UK/Irish Collection below). To access the majority of the information you need to take out a subscription, though there are sections that are free, so it is worth exploring even if you're not planning to subscribe. The availability of the US census must be one of the key reasons for joining if you can make use of it.

A word of warning about the cancelling of subscriptions, including a 'free 14-day trial' for which you need to hand over your credit card details. You are told to unsubscribe by dialling a toll-free number in Utah, which will not work from outside the US. The alternative is to phone a Utah-based telephone number, which can prove both expensive and frustrating. Although it is difficult to find mention of it on the site, international customers (that is, those outside the US) can email **support@ancestry-inc.com** to cancel. You must provide your full name, email address, username and say that you are an international customer. Even then, reports suggest that it is still worth checking your credit card statement to ensure that your subscription has been cancelled.

The homepage is quite busy and cluttered. The prominent search box that greets you is not a bad place to start, or use the tabs across the top of the page to get to the section you want. In general, navigation is quite obscure with no obvious way of navigating back to lists once you follow a link, though a Site Tour is available from the Site Help link at the bottom of the homepage, and then from the FAQs list.

SPECIAL FEATURES

Search lets you put in a first and second name, or simply a surname, specify a locality or not as you choose, and then press the search button. This will almost certainly produce a good number of hits depending, of course, on how specific you have been and how unusual the name is. To progress further you will either need to pay or, at the very least, sign up as a 'guest', for which you have to give your email address. The risk of having a cluttered inbox thereafter is obvious.

Genealogy Search by Location allows you to select 'UK and Ireland' or, from a map of the British Isles, also Scotland, Wales, the Channel Islands and the Isle of Man. The resulting lists look impressive at first glance, but much of the material on offer is very general and repetitive, such as in the Biography & History sections, where lists of British peerage and the landed gentry are given. The UK and Irish material includes parish and probate records, the Irish

Famine Index, Pallot's Marriages and Baptisms. Access to these can be obtained by buying an annual UK/Ireland subscription at $69.95 per annum, and thereafter you will be billed quarterly. If you are already a subscriber you can add these new databases for $29.95. Before signing up though it is worth taking a close look at what records are available as they are by no means comprehensive. Checking by county you may find that they have only one or two parish registers relating to the area you're interested in, or some marriage licence details for a very small time period. More records are likely to be added regularly but it has some way to go before this is more than a hit and miss affair for UK researchers. The references to UK Civil Registration records are true but somewhat misleading: Ancestry.com hosts a copy of the FreeBMD database (see p. 56), which is located on RootsWeb, but if you access via Ancestry.com, which offers a better search facility, you can still reach these records for free, without needing to subscribe.

Genealogy Help introduces various family history resources, principally the Ancestry Library, which could be useful. Articles from the archives of Ancestry Magazine can be accessed without a subscription.

Family Trees provides much of the data for the site, with individuals posting their personal information on the Message Boards (the adjacent tab), contributing to the Ancestry World Tree or joining the Research Registry. This is where the possibility for unreliable information is inevitably introduced. Here you are also offered online website space for your family tree and a means of staying in touch with your family worldwide. The software provided online is increasingly sophisticated and flexible in the reports it can produce, and if you are collaborating with someone elsewhere the ability to share your information online is attractive.

Ancestry Shops takes you to publications, software packages and other products of interest to researchers, all for sale at the click of a button, and gives you the opportunity to sign up for the ProductWatch newsletter. Be aware that using this US-based facility will probably mean incurring import taxes and will certainly involve carriage costs.

FamilyHistory.com and MyFamily.com are both associated websites, which are accessible from within this website.

This is a real curate's egg: if they've got what you want it can be very useful, but the chances of UK researchers finding pertinent information here remain fairly low, and that has to be weighed against the costs of subscribing. Try other places first.

Civil Registration

Confusingly, the civil registration records are known on some sites as BMDs and others at BDMs, and on others still as Vital Records. Either way, they cover records of births, marriages and deaths. Civil registrations provide the most reliable sources of information on ancestors from when registration began (1837 in England and Wales, although it was not compulsory until 1875). For Scottish and Irish registrations see Chapter 4.

It is not possible to view the actual certificates (apart from samples) anywhere on the web, or indeed in person, without ordering the certificates either from the FRC or the ONS or a local records office (see reviews in Chapter 2). The cost of certificates starts at £6.50. However, the extra information to be gained from the certificates makes this worth doing if you have managed to trace the reference for the event. For example, you might have found the date of a wedding on the FreeBMD site, but a certificate will reveal the names and occupations of the bride and groom's fathers, the couple's occupations, marital status, ages (or whether they were 'of full age') and address at the time of marriage, the names of two witnesses, whether the couple were married by banns or licence (the latter would lead you to further documentation) and the name of the place in which they were married. Previously the only way to obtain a certificate, unless you already knew the exact details, was to obtain a GRO reference either by visiting the FRC or its predecessors, or consulting the indexes on fiche at a local records office or FHC. The following sites provide increasingly viable alternatives.

http://freebmd.rootsweb.com
FreeBMD

Overall rating: ★ ★ ★ ★ ★

Classification:	Records	Readability:	★ ★ ★ ★
Updating:	Monthly	Content:	★ ★ ★ ★
Navigation:	★ ★ ★ ★ ★	Speed:	★ ★ ★ ★

UK

When the first edition of this guide went to print, the Free BMD project was noted as a promising seedling within the mighty RootsWeb, as the database at that time had fewer than two million entries. Today it contains over 50 million records (double the number since the last edition of this guide), all transcribed by volunteers, and its value to family historians grows by the month as more are added. It provides free online access to the indexes of births, marriages and deaths recorded under the Civil Registration process. You can't view the actual certificates online, but in many cases it provides a very useful shortcut to the full registration details, which makes it cheaper to buy the certificates.

Inevitably there are still many gaps, as a look at Information, Statistics and then Database Coverage will indicate. As a result, you may not find the person you're looking for at all, or for a marriage you may only find the partner whose name starts with a letter closer to the beginning of the alphabet. However, these caveats are outweighed by the usefulness of searching the records in such a flexible way: an infinite improvement over consulting microfiche or the big quarterly volumes. Because the results show the occurrences of names over a spread of years, it can also be a useful way of spotting potential siblings, particularly if a surname is quite rare in a particular part of the country. You will need to follow up other sources to prove a connection, but a little study can suggest many missing links.

SPECIAL FEATURES

Search First-time users may find it worth taking the offer of a fuller explanation of how to get the most out of your search, with a link just under the heading. None of the boxes is compulsory, but if your search is too vague, FreeBMD won't be able to cope. Choose between All Types, Births, Deaths and Marriages. Cut down the number of results by specifying start and end dates for your search, and the districts or counties if known. Use asterisks and question marks to denote missing or unknown characters. Although you are offered the option of completing a spouse's details, it is probably best to ignore this: it may be that the spouse has not yet been entered onto the system, and you increase the chances of variant spellings preventing the database from finding the original ancestor. Once you've got the search results, you can click through on the page number to see the names of other people whose details appear on the same page of the register. One of these may be the spouse of the person you are looking for. Or do a separate search if you already know the name of a spouse.

Join FreeBMD provides details of how to sign up to be a transcriber on this worthile project.

Transcribers Page Even if you're not a transcriber it can be worth checking out this page, as it provides very useful graphs showing the coverage of each type of record by year. This can be helpful in deciding next steps when a search is unsuccessful: is the birth not found in the year you expected because someone has been lying about their age, or because only 2% of the births from that year have been subscribed? In general, coverage of marriages is by far the most advanced, with some years approaching 100%, births are patchy and deaths have barely been started.

This is a great resource, a model of what the internet can do, and the project deserves the support of as many volunteers as possible, so that it reaches completeness sooner.

---

www.ancestry.com/search/rectype/vital/freebmd
FreeBMD at Ancestry.com

★★★★ US

The data from the FreeBMD project can now be accessed via the site of RootsWeb's sponsor, Ancestry.com, where it hides under the title of England Wales, Civil Registration Index: 1837-1900. Although they list this facility as one of the advantages of taking out their new UK and Ireland subsciption package, you do not have to subscribe to view it. Ancestry.com has a faster server than RootsWeb and the search facility will perform more complex searches than FreeBMD allows (for example a forename without a surname). One drawback is that you have to either specify a single year or leave the field blank, rather than searching a range of years as you can on the FreeBMD. Also, early reports suggest that the Ancestry.com interface is having problems differentiating between registration districts and confusing those that start with the same three letters. Our tip is to use it for your initial searches, but make sure you cross-check with either FreeBMD or the original GRO indexes before trying to order certificates from the registration details provided.

www.ukbdm.org.uk

The UK BDM (Births, Deaths and Marriages) Exchange

Overall rating: ★ ★ ★ ★			
Classification: Name-search		**Readability:**	★ ★ ★ ★
Updating: Regularly		**Content:**	★ ★ ★
Navigation: ★ ★ ★ ★		**Speed:**	★ ★ ★ ★

UK

Another great idea, flawed only by the incompleteness of the data and reliance on volunteers – so take this as a call to action! It is a free resource, putting you in touch with other genealogists and listing the BDM certificates they hold. If you spend a few minutes posting the details of certificates you have in your possession, other researchers can email you for details rather than having to buy a copy of the certificate themselves. You, in turn, may be able to benefit from the researches of others. It also works as a surname listing, putting you in touch with people who have same-name interests as you in the same geographical areas.

To understand more about the object of the service, click first on Help in the purple buttons to the left of the homepage. If this button is not immediately on view (it is near the bottom of the list), scroll down on the adjacent bar. The page that now comes up is headed How to Navigate the UK BDM Exchange. Before navigating, however, you still need to understand what the site is trying to do. Click on About (in blue lettering at the bottom of the page), and at last you get answers.

SPECIAL FEATURES

Use the purple buttons down the left-hand side of the page to select from a list including **Births, Deaths, Marriages, Baptisms, Burials** and **ParMarr** (Parish Marriages), and then click on the relevant letter of the alphabet from the bar along the bottom of the page to see if anyone is researching the name you are interested in. If you know a maiden, but not a married, name, click on **Wives**, which may produce the married name you need, in which case return to one of the earlier lists.

If you find a record you want to consult further, contact the researcher at the address indicated. Those certificates that have proved irrelevant or are no longer wanted have a 'Y' beside them, meaning that the researcher in question is prepared to pass them on. Researchers will still give information, of course, even where the actual certificates are being retained, so if you have any certificates of your own that you are prepared to share or pass on, register here!

This service, set up in 1997, is an excellent idea and a very necessary one. Previous problems with slow speeds seem to have improved considerably, though you can still wait a while for particularly long pages to load fully.

http://iigs.rootsweb.com/bdm

International Internet Genealogical Society BDM Exchange

★ ★ ★ ★   US

Working on the same principle as the UK BDM Exchange, this sites has lists for many different countries, though not all are well used as yet. The list includes Irish (EI), Canadian, Australian and New Zealand. You need to scroll down the page to find the actual links, which take the form of abbreviations of the countries listed in the index at the top of the page.

Parish records

When you've managed to trace your ancestors back to before the civil registration process began in 1837 (or even back to the early years, before it became compulsory in 1875) the events recorded in parish registers provide the main source of vital records. Note that these record baptisms, rather than births (although the latter may also be included) and that there may be a long time lapse between birth and baptism. Some families had several children baptised at the same time, and other people were baptised as adults, so baptismal dates are not always reliable clues to age. Most Church of England parish registers are lodged with local records offices, although some recent ones are still in use in the churches. Many have also been filmed by the LDS and can be searched on their online database at familysearch.com or found in their supplementary CD-Roms called the BVRI, which can be consulted at FRCs or bought on CD rom (see p.37).

The SoG (p.41) has the largest collection of transcripts and indexes of parish registers from all around the UK, and you can check their holdings online at www.sog.org.uk.

Many nonconformists had to be married in the Church of England for their marriage to be recognised. For details of Roman Catholic and nonconformist records see pp. 121-22.

As well as the sites listed below as having parish transcripts for sale, take a look at the sites selling software and data CDs in chapter 9.

There are many partial transcriptions available on the internet but not collected together in a systematic way; look under the county pages on GENUKI or search on Google.

www.familysearch.org
IGI at Family search

★★★★★ US

The most comprehensive set of parish register transcriptions on the internet. For full review, see p.36. To check which parish registers are included in the database use the Place Search in the Family History Library Catalogue.

www.sog.org.uk/prc/index.html
Society of Genealogists

★★★★★ UK

Check their online catalogue to see whether they hold transcripts of the registers you are interested in among the SoG's collection of over 11,000 register copies.

www.englishorigins.com
English Origins

★★★★★ UK R

The main material of interest here is Boyd's Marriage Index, covering 1.5 million names from East Anglian parishes between 1538 and 1840. There is also a Marriage Licence Allegations Index covering 670,00 names, with details of intended marriages where the couples preferred the speed and discretion of swearing that there was no impediment to their forthcoming marriage, rather than waiting for the banns to be read on three consecutive Sundays. For the full review of the Origins site, see p.31.

http://freereg.rootsweb.com
FreeREG

★★★★ UK

Like the FreeBMD project, this relies on an army of volunteers to transcribe the parish registers into three databases: baptisms, marriages and burials. Unfortunately the databases are not yet searchable, but there is still valuable, explanatory information here, and so it is worth checking back regularly for a progress report.

English and Welsh Parish Registers provides a useful introduction to the subject giving descriptions of English Parish Registers for baptisms, marriages and burials.

http://freereg.rootsweb.com/howto/latinwords.htm is part of the same site, and provides a useful list of Latin words and phrases you will come across in the older parish records.

www.ancestry.com
Ancestry.com

★★★★★ US £

You need to subscribe to the UK and Irish records to view Pallot's Marriage and Baptism Indexes 1780-1837, plus random selections from parish and probate records. See p.53.

www.ihgs.ac.uk
Institute of Heraldry and Genealogical Studies

★★★ UK

The IHGS has the Sussex collection of parish registers available for sale on microfiche. See also p.170

www.ffhs.org.uk
Federation of Family History Societies

★★★ UK

Use this site to reach the individual FHSs, many of which have compiled and published transcripts of parishes within their area. These are usually available on microfiche, sometimes in printed form. You can also purchase the National Burial Index for England and Wales on CD-rom by following the links from this site. Full review on p.40.

http://prtsoc.org.uk
The Parish Register Transcription Society

★★★ UK

Publishers of a range of transcripts of parish registers, available on microfilm. Hampshire, Norfolk, West Sussex and the Isle of Wight are the most comprehensively covered.

www.curiousfox.com
Curious Fox

★★★ UK

Because so much genealogical research is, in the preliminary stages, place-related rather than person-related, this relatively new website takes town or village names as its starting point and invites submissions accordingly. You can search for free but membership offers more benefits. The star rating above reflects the fact that the site is slow to load and its data is, as yet, limited, but it could grow into something very big and very good.

Census records

Finding a branch of your family in a census is like hitting the jackpot: at best you will discover all the members of the family group who were living together at that time, where they lived, how many people they shared the premises with, whether there were servants, lodgers or other family members living there, their names, ages, occupations, relationship to head of household, marital status, and where they were born. Of course, not all of these details may be available, legible, or reliable.

And there are other problems: although the first census was taken in 1801 it is only from the 1841 census onwards that individual data was collected. And as records are not released to the public for 100 years, the 1901 census is the most recent one available.

The other main difficulty in finding your family is that the original records are organised by addresses within an enumeration district. Most of the censuses have a fairly basic street index, available at the FRC or wherever there are copies of the census, but name indexes are much rarer. 1881 is the best served, fully indexed on CD-rom and searchable by forenames, surnames, occupations and addresses. The new 1901 census has also been transcribed and is searchable online, and there are several projects underway to index 1891. For earlier censuses, what indexes there are tend to be very localised, the fruits of the labours of local family history societies or dedicated individuals.

Handwriting in the original census documents is frequently very difficult to read, and so transcriptions may not be accurate. In the absence of relevant indexes, you need to start with known addresses suggested by BDM certificates and trawl through likely areas page by page.

Although the service is now available, testing it with a number of names that should have produced immediate results only revealed considerable 'holes'. The frustration is that the online method of access is now the only one available, if you wish to search by name. Your only alternative is to search by place, on microfiche at the FRC.

www.census.pro.gov.uk		
Census Online		
Overall rating: ★★★★		
Classification: Records	**Readability:**	★★★★
Updating: Regularly	**Content:**	★★★★
Navigation: ★★★★	**Speed:**	★★★★
UK £ 🔒		

The PRO launched its project to put the UK censuses online with the 1901 records that became open to the public in January 2002. The digitising of the 1891 census is underway and negotiations to use the work already done on the 1881 census are in progress. The launch of this service attracted wide media coverage, and the system could not cope with the millions trying to log on.

SPECIAL FEATURES

Search The options here are Person Search, Advanced Person, Place, Insitution, Vessel or Direct Search. Address Search will be added in due course. Up to this point these searches are free. In each of these there are several boxes to help narrow your search (such as age, place of birth, or place keywords), though it is better to do a broader search first and then narrow down the options if you get too many results, as you can easily miss the right person if you specify information that does not agree with the transcribed entry. The search only copes with one 'First Name', so if you know with certainty of more than one name you should use the Advanced Person Search and use the Other Names box. The results pages give you basic details from which you can work out which of the records you want to view. To view either the full transcription or the original census record (as a scanned document) you are transferred to a payment screen.

Account Sessions There are two ways of paying to view the records: by credit card or vouchers obtainable in multiples of £5 from the FRC, PRO, SoG and many family history societies. The minimum session costs £5 either way, but whereas you have up to six months to use up a voucher after you first register it, a credit-card session must be used within 48 hours. This restriction caused large problems in the busy first days after the site went live and people could not get access and so the period had to be extended; it may be that the PRO caves in to public pressure to keep this extension, but check on the site for latest information. Either way, it is likely that using vouchers is a better option unless you have an intensive period to set aside for your research. If you do use a credit card, you are able to specify an upper limit. Setting this quite high is worthwhile because, when you have reached your specified limit, if you decide to continue, your new session will be subject to the £5 minimum limit again. Make sure that you suspend your session rather than logging off when you have finished so that can you resume later. Don't forget to make a note of your unique session ID. Session Details will show you what you have spent, and what you have left.

Viewing an individual's transcription costs 50p, and you can then choose to view either the transcriptions of all others in the household for a further 50p, or go straight to the original census image (which will probably reveal all the other household members) for 75p. Once downloaded, the images can be stored on your hard disk, or printed out. The site advises printing on A3, good advice but not a facility that all home-based users will have. There are good zoom facilities

for viewing the image, and you can reverse the colours to see it white on black, which is often easier for deciphering difficult handwriting.

Tour this Site The site is quite straightforward to use, but if you are daunted, take the clear site demo tour first.

Many have objected to the principle of paying for public records, though the ability to do so from your home PC is convenient. The worrying feature is the frustration of identifying evident gaps in the data and the annoying message 'your search is taking too long' when the search facility can't cope, presumably as a result of poor transcription.

www.steeljam.co.uk/1901census/1901/html
1901 Census

★★★ (UK)

Explanation is given here of the Census page reference system and how to make use of it.

http://1891-census.co.uk/index.html
1891 Census

★★★★　UK

It is early days as yet for the digitisation of the 1891 UK Census. At time of writing only Oxfordshire is both imaged and indexed, though Dorset, Cambridgeshire, Nottinghamshire and Lincolnshire are not far behind. Ancestry.co.uk is the host and is offering a free 14-day trial. This has the potential rapidly to become a five-star resource.

http://county-surnames.co.uk
UK Surnames

★★★★　UK

Malcolm Hills has created a major surname database here, divided by county, or region for Scotland, Wales and Ireland. There is a section dedicated to 1901 Census Transcription Errors. To find this, enter the site as a Non-Member and scroll down the resulting page to near the bottom.

http://web.ukonline.co.uk/sheila.jones/ppp.htm
Sheila's Site

★★★★　UK

Sheila Jones gives a general introduction to UK censuses and provides indexes with full personal details for the 2% survey of the 1851 census. Each county is indexed separately and the indexes come as zipped files which can be downloaded to read offline. Although 98% of the population is missing, it is worth investigating what could prove a very useful shortcut to finding your ancestors. Replace 'ceninfo'

in the URL with 'strays1' to find lists of people who were outside their countries of birth at the time of the census.

At the date of this edition of this guide, the website was undergoing a complete upgrade, so a lot of information was temporarily unavailable.

www.gendocs.demon.co.uk
Gendocs

★★★★　UK

This fascinating website has a definite London bias, though there is UK-wide material too. It provides a handy list of the details recorded in each census, and the dates they were taken on (scroll down the page to view them all), as well as links to other general information such as a list of all the London Census Surname Indexes available for purchase or look-up by Clive Ayton.

www.censuslinks.com
Census Links

★★★　US

An international listings site with links to transcribed records all over the world.

www.genealogy.demon.co.uk
S & N Genealogy

★★★　UK

S & N have started digitising original census records and releasing them on sets of CD-roms and DVDs. These are not.

indexed (apart from somewhat unreliable street indexes), though on release of the first set of discs, for London 1891, volunteers immediately started a transcription project, and there are plans to release the index on CD-rom and online as soon as it becomes available. See also p. 149.

The London 1901 Census is now available on CD (45 CDs in total costing £59.95, for a limited period) and, as a look at the sample pages will show, it is immeasurably clearer than the online version, especially if you click on the magnifier icon, then hover your mouse over the part of the page that interests you and click repeatedly. Volunteers are already indexing by name and this will be available on CD in due course

www.lds.org.uk/genealogy/software.htm
Latter-Day Saints Online

★★★   UK

Use this link to find ordering details of the wonderful set of CD-roms with the fully searchable index to the 1881 census for England and Wales, and the 1851 census for Devon, Norfolk and Warwickshire.

Wills

www.pro-online.pro.gov.uk
PRO Online

★★★★★ UK

The PRO has started to put its collection of Registered Copies of Wills from 1383 to 1858 online. At the time of writing only a fraction of these were accessible, all from 1740 onwards and so far still incomplete, but the ease of use of the system and reasonable price (£3) for downloading a copy of a will in a PDF format make this a very welcome service. There are also three leaflets about wills, probate and death duty records on the main www.pro.gov.uk site.

www.englishorigins.com
English Origins

★★★★★ UK £ 🔒

From this site you can search the indexes for, and order copies of, the original documents from the Bank of England Will Extracts 1717-1845 with over 60,000 entries, and you can also access the Archdeaconry Court of London Wills Index 1700-1807, and the Prerogative Court of Canterbury Wills Index 1750-1800 (incomplete). See p.31 for a full review and details of charges. This site provides details of how and where to access wills made after 1858. Society of Genealogists members get free access for one 48-hour period each quarter (non-members pay £6) and other discounts.

www.genuki.org.uk/big/eng/Probate.html
England Probate Records

★★★★★ UK

A good overview of what records are available, with links to the places online where records can be found.

**www.courtservice.gov.uk/wills_probate/
probate_famhist.htm**
Court Service

★★★ UK

This site has details of where to apply for copies of post-1858 wills. Find this under Using the Courts, then Wills & Probate, then A Guide to Obtaining Probate Records.

Obituaries

Although obituaries can be a rich hunting ground for family historians, very few are available online, and the majority of those are either American or very recent, covering the period from the early 1990s. To track down older or local newspapers that might have carried a reference try consulting the British Library's newspaper collection catalogue on http://prodigi.bl.uk/nlcat (see p.143).

www.rootsweb.com/~obituary
The Obituary Daily Times

★★★ US

An army of contributors regularly scour their local (mainly American) newpapers and index the obituaries. You can subscribe to the mailing list, to be sent emails twice a day, or search the archive online. The site doesn't hold the actual reviews, but the listings provide enough information to allow you to find the source. If you contribute to the site, other contributors will trade or may send you the actual review you need.

www.obitcentral.com/obitsearch
Obituary Archive Search Engine

★★★ US

There are lots of links here to obituary sites around the world, but the site is difficult to navigate and there are distracting advertisements. Relatively little for non-Americans.

www.telegraph.co.uk
The Telegraph

★★★ US

Select Obituaries from the menu list on the left of the homepage to be taken to the most recent entry, or you can search the archive back to 1994.

http://news.independent.co.uk/people/obituaries
The Independent Obituaries

★★★ UK

The archive only dates back to 1999, but this is a simple-to-use and well-written set of memorials.

www.guardian.co.uk
The Guardian

★★★ UK

Use the powerful Archive Search facility to find obituaries that have appeared in either The Guardian or The Observer since 1998.

www.newsint-archive.co.uk
The Times and Sunday Times archive

★★★ UK £

The £10 minimum buys you ten pages of articles from the Times' and Sunday Times' searchable archive, dating back to 1984. The last seven days' obituaries can be viewed for free on www.thetimes.co.uk. Use Frequently Asked Questions for more information.

Passenger Lists

The web is awash with transcriptions of passenger lists. Try the following for a comprehensive set of links.

www.scan.org.uk/knowledgebase/topics/topicpassengerlists.htm
Knowledge Base

★★★★★ UK

Although Knowledge Base is part of the Scottish Archive Network, it provides the best general introduction to searching Passenger Lists for America, Canada, Australia and New Zealand.

www.cyndislist.com/ships.htm
Cyndi's List Ships and Passenger list

★★★★★ US

As ever, Cyndi comes up trumps with an exhaustive and well-classified set of links. Good listings also for seamen as well as passengers.

http://members.aol.com/rprost/passenger.html
Passenger Lists on the Internet

★★★★ US

The basic presentation should not deter you from investigating this well-maintained set of links. It scores by giving brief descriptions of the sites.

http://istg.rootsweb.com
Immigrant Ships Transcribers Guild

★★★★ US

Although there is no search facility here, this simple site is quite straightforward to navigate. You can access the lists of passenger names by date of departure, ship's name, port of departure or port of arrival. Follow the link to The Compass for a very good set of links to other lists and information about ships and migration generally.

http://olivetreegenealogy.com
Olive Tree Genealogy

★★★★ US

Too many of the links on this site lead you straight back to pay sites such as ancestry.com (usually indicated by an Off Site button), but select Search Ships Lists in the tabs near the top of the Databases page and you'll find the lists hosted at the Olive Tree.

Surname Lists

The idea is a simple one: lists of the names people are researching, along with details of the area and approximate time frame, plus the contact details of the person submitting the entry. What differentiates the various lists is obviously how well used they are, how easy it is to submit your details, whether you can search, and most importantly whether someone who shares your research interests stumbles across the same surname board. It is worth checking all of these (and any others you come across) every few months, just in case. The frequency of Late Sixteenth Century Given Names is studied in a few interesting pages at www. s-gabriel.org/names/talan/eng16

www.genuki.org.uk/indexes/SurnamesLists.html
GENUKI Index of Surname Lists

★★★★★ UK

Many of the county-specific surname lists that were once hosted by GENUKI have now been consolidated under the master lists maintained by Graham Jaunay as the Online Names Research Directory (see previous review), which you can also access from this page. Links to those that remain independent can be found here, as well as links to Isle of Man and Channel Islands boards.

http://rsl.rootsweb.com
RootsWeb Surname Lists

★★★★ US R

To make a post on this international but American dominated list, you first have to set up an eight-character nametag, which is easier said than done if you have anything like a reasonably common name (best to have something pretty obscure up your sleeve before you start). Luckily there is a facility to be reminded of forgotten nametags. Entries are added immediately. You don't need to be registered to search the list, which is by means of a search box. This is quick and efficient but it can be frustrating not being able to browse (though the sheer numbers registered here would make that rather a bore). However, a useful feature when you get a match is the ability to view all the other surnames submitted by that submitter. You can also choose to view only recent updates, so you don't have to trawl through the same records every time you search.

Register now for FREE online updates

Simply log on to www.thegoodwebguide.co.uk
or fill in your details and return this registration card to us

guide title	
your name	
address	
postcode	
email	

Would you like information on any of the following Good Web Guides? Please tick.

- [ ] sport
- [ ] tv
- [ ] gay life
- [ ] comedy
- [ ] wine
- [ ] money
- [ ] genealogy
- [ ] gardening
- [ ] food
- [ ] music
- [ ] sex
- [ ] games
- [ ] home
- [ ] travel
- [ ] health
- [ ] parents
- [ ] museums & art galleries
- [ ] antiques & collectables
- [ ] world religons
- [ ] gambling
- [ ] the good web guide

2

Marketing Department
The Good Web Guide
65 Bromfelde Road
LONDON
SW4 6BR

Look-up Exchanges

These sites maintain lists of reference works or databases owned by individuals who are willing to look up surnames or other information for enquirers. It is important to recognise that these are all volunteers with their own busy lives and research interests, so be patient and polite, and most importantly be very precise about your request. Asking for all the Smiths listed is not likely to get you very far. The resources on offer can be enormously varied, including census indexes, street atlases, trade directories such as Pigot's and Kelly's, and post office directories, apprenticeship records, parish registers, gazetteers, marriage licence allegations, passenger lists and monumental inscriptions. The operative word here is Exchange: if you have benefited from the kindness of strangers and have something to offer, submit it.

http://www.lookupcentral.f9.co.uk/volunteers.html
County Lookup Exchange Central

★★★★★ UK

This website, which replaces the former Lookup Exchange, leads to county by county listings for England and Wales. The Scottish equivalent seems, unfortunately, to have disappeared but the Isle of Man version has moved to **www.isle-of-man.com/interests/genealogy/look-up.htm.**

www.raogk.org
Random Acts of Genealogical Kindness

★★★★ US

Volunteers around the world agree to perform one look-up request per month in their area, from photographing tombstones, houses and schools to searching in local records offices, or checking references in books and resources they have at home. You are expected to reimburse direct costs and to be willing to reciprocate by volunteering your own efforts. Certainly, sites like these restore your faith in human nature and make you want to give something back to the online community.

One-name Studies

www.one-name.org
Guild of One-Name Studies

Overall rating: ★ ★ ★ ★			
Classification:	Research	**Readability:**	★ ★ ★ ★
Updating:	Occasionally	**Content:**	★ ★ ★
Navigation:	★ ★ ★	**Speed:**	★ ★ ★

UK

For anyone interested in following up research through a one-name studies website, GOONS will be the best place to start, precisely because it is UK-based. Note that a one-name study seeks to research all occurrences of a single surname, not to follow a particular family tree. Note also that the only method of return to the homepage, or indeed any other, is the 'back' button on the top toolbar.

SPECIAL FEATURES

Services Available to Members explains that The Guild Email Forum, free permanent email addresses and access to the Biography Database 1680–1830 are all restricted to members.

Research Facilities for Members and Non-Members explains how requesting help from Guild Members, who all give their services voluntarily, is made easier if you ask specific rather than general questions and are patient about response times.

The Online Searchable Register of One Name Studies contains details of over 7000 studies, accessible either by alphabetical listings or inserting a name in the search box. Each entry gives contact details for the compiler including email addresses where available. It can be very instructive to see the variants of names listed, as these give clues to alternative spellings to look for.

Given that there is nowhere near enough space in this book to list one-name sites individually, your best route to exploring whether there is anything in them for you is probably to start here. That way you can take advantage of the good explanation of what one-name sites are and how to contribute. It probably makes sense to do a quick search and then use Cyndi's List if you want to try further afield.

Submitted data

These consist of sites or services drawing on family trees that individual researchers have submitted or posted on the internet. As such, the reliability of the data can be extremely variable and the responsible family historian will always use the information to check the original sources, rather than relying on it without question.

Many of these sites display surname-search boxes and other links promising to search millions of names, which inevitably lead you back to Ancestry.com or Genealogy.com, providing income for the referring site. You will soon get used to spotting these links (and usually ignoring them) as you surf around.

Because there are so many American genealogists online, you will find that the majority of records you come across are US based, but of course the picture is changing as the genealogy bug spreads around the world. It's up to all of us to start putting our own data up there for other genealogists to find, and then more will follow suit. So don't necessarily dismiss a site just because of an American bias: colonise it!

It is wonderful to come across someone else who is researching some of the same lines as you, and it is this prospect that keeps people submitting their data to these sites. But you may be just as likely to come across their web pages by searching relevant surname boards (see p.66) or typing the names of your ancestors into Google (see p. 132) so do some exploring, and certainly use the demos on paid-for sites before committing your money.

www.gencircles.com
GenCircles.com

Overall rating: ★ ★ ★ ★			
Classification:	General	Readability:	★ ★ ★ ★
Updating:	Occasionally	Content:	★ ★ ★ ★
Navigation:	★ ★ ★ ★	Speed:	★ ★ ★ ★

US R

Registered users submit their family histories as GEDCOM files. The resulting 'Global Tree' index can be easily and flexibly searched. When you view the results of the search, the simple key shows you whether an individual has descendants within the database, whether there are notes on the individual, and whether the sources of the information are cited.

SPECIAL FEATURES

SmartMatching One of the major incentives for submitting your tree is the facility that runs a detailed search on every individual in your file, and to see where your names match up with individuals in other people's files.

Clubs When you run a search on a surname, the results alert to you whether there is a surname club of people who are also interested in that name.

Global Tree allows you to adminster your uploaded GEDCOM files, by updating or deleting them online.

Cliff Shaw who developed Gen Forum and now Gen Circles, has launched a software product called Family Tree Legends, offering automatic online back-up, GEDCOM publishing with instant updates and smart-matching as standard.

The great functionality of this site and responsible attitude to members' data deserve to make this a success. If more Brits used it, it could be an extremely valuable resource.

www.gendex.com
GENDEX

Overall rating: ★ ★ ★			
Classification:	Name-search	**Readability:**	★ ★ ★ ★
Updating:	Occasionally	**Content:**	★ ★ ★
Navigation:	★ ★ ★ ★	**Speed:**	★ ★ ★

US R £ 🔒

Gendex doesn't hold all the data on the site, but provides an index of the names that appear on thousands of websites across the world wide web, and allows you to contact the data owners.

SPECIAL FEATURES

GENDEX-WWW Genealogical Index offers three ways of searching: by surname, prefix of surname, and with a facility that delivers variant spellings. If you have registered, you can perform more sophisticated searches. By registering you also receive 100 free 'hit credits', and further hit credits can be prepaid for $10 per thousand. Also offered is an index of individuals who don't have a surname, as well as a list of surnames 'beginning with characters outside the range A–Z'.

GED2HTML This little programme is very useful for converting genealogical data into HTML web pages, complete with hyperlinks. If you are using one of the online family tree programs you are not usually given the option of exporting your data as a GEDCOM file, but this software will allow you to convert it.

Genealogical web page storage can be rented for a 'modest' fee starting at $2 per year. After 25Mb of storage, though, the rates rise sharply.

More useful if you know you have American connections, but worth a try anyway.

www.gensource.com
Gensource.com

Overall rating: ★ ★ ★			
Classification:	General	**Readability:**	★ ★ ★
Updating:	Occasionally	**Content:**	★ ★ ★ ★ ★
Navigation:	★ ★	**Speed:**	★ ★ ★

US

Gensource contains three major databases, collating a large number of genealogy websites submitted by individual genealogists. Ignore the first search box on the home page, which is an advertisement for Ancestry.com (see p.53). The actual Gensource service is free.

SPECIAL FEATURES

Common Threads puts individuals researching the same family name in touch with each other. It is aimed at helping those who have reached a 'dead end' in their search. You can Add Your Ancestor and Update your Entry as needed by following the prompts. Good information about the service is found under Descriptions and FAQs. When inputting names, you should use 'and' to link the parts of the name (for instance, 'John and Henry and Smith').

I Found it! is a database of genealogy websites in many different categories, searchable by keywords. A brief test suggested that keeping the search simple would be necessary.

I Found it! Archives, meanwhile, is a growing list of actual archives that have been transcribed onto the internet by individuals and can, consequently, be consulted online.

If you have really run into a brick wall in your research, this would certainly be one place to flag up your difficulty in the hope that some other individual might be able to help out.

www.genserv.com

GenServ Genealogical GEDCOM Server System

Overall rating: ★ ★ ★			
Classification:	Name-search	**Readability:**	★ ★
Updating:	Occasionally	**Content:**	★ ★
Navigation:	★ ★	**Speed:**	★ ★ ★

US R £ 🔒

This very cluttered, very confusing, very colourful site is daunting, to say the least, though a little persistence may be rewarded. A free trial membership is possible for an introductory period, after which a modest subscription is charged. The site is run by Cliff Manis from Texas. In Suffolk he has a colleague named Jon Rees who handles European membership and postal queries. What Cliff has created is a database of individual GEDCOM files, to which you can add your own and through which you can consult others. Communications from GenServ are made to you via email.

SPECIAL FEATURES

How to Join GenServ outlines four steps, the first of which is 'Create a GEDCOM file', and then gives three further stages for submitting it. Full access is denied until a GEDCOM file has been submitted. If creating a GEDCOM file is a new task, select Documentation from the yellow tabs near the top of the homepage and then scroll down to GEDMAKE, last in the list on that page.

Very repetitive, this site keeps going round in circles and is not immediately easy to use, but there are good things in here and you may just happen upon another user who is researching the same family tree. Worth a try.

Have you registered for free updates?

log on to
www.thegoodweguide.co.uk

Chapter 4

regional resources
for britain & ireland

Once you have traced your ancestors to a particular part of the country, perhaps by finding the place of birth in a census record, a whole range of new places to search opens up. Many records are held in local or county records offices, which could be well worth visiting, and we list sites that will help you find out where they are and what they hold. Even though you can consult censuses and some parish records online, on CDs or at the main London-based records offices, local holdings can be invaluable for putting some flesh on the bones of names and dates. To find the parish church where your ancestors were baptised, married or buried, to see if their names appear on the village war memorial, whether they qualified for poor-law help, what sort of industry they would have been involved in: all aspects of their lives can be better understood in a local context. There are so many local sites that space

prevents us from dealing with individual counties in depth. We therefore start off with some sites that provide gateways to local information. London, however, is covered in considerable detail, partly because of the richness of the resources held there, but also because so many researchers will have at least one line that has passed through the capital at some time.

After London, we deal with Ireland, Northern Ireland, Scotland and Wales, the Channel Islands and Isle of Man.

Two of the very best places to start regional research have already been discussed. RootsWeb and GENUKI have in-depth resources, organised by county, and should be among your first ports of call after you've tracked your ancestors down in a particular area.

www.familia.org.uk
Familia

Overall rating: ★ ★ ★ ★ ★			
Classification:	Libraries	**Readability:**	★ ★ ★ ★ ★
Updating:	Regularly	**Content:**	★ ★ ★ ★ ★
Navigation:	★ ★ ★ ★	**Speed:**	★ ★ ★ ★

UK

Familia is a web-based directory of family history resources held in public libraries in the UK and Ireland.

SPECIAL FEATURES

Libraries Index Click on the region you want to see an overview of the main collections, opening hours and types of records available. The local authorities that appear in italics have not submitted details of their holdings.

Maps and Places helps you find places if you don't know what local authority they come under.

Guides suggest where to go next for information depending on what you know about your ancestors.

Sources has excellent brief explanations of what will be found in, for instance, Census Returns, Parish Registers or Electoral Registers and Poll Books.

Links produces a useful list of connections to, for example, the Association of Genealogists and Researchers in Archives at www.agra.org.uk (see p. 169) and the very useful MultiMap (see p. 138), which lets you pinpoint UK towns and villages, even if you do not know which county they are in, as well as London streets and GB postcode areas.

This simple, unflashy website has many uses, principally the directory of library contents but also some useful links.

www.genuki.org.uk/mindex.html
UK & Ireland Genealogy

★ ★ ★ ★ ★ UK

This page gives links to all the county genealogy listings for the UK (as well as including comprehensive indexes of one-name studies, family history societies and mailing lists), and there are detailed contents for each county. You will need to scroll down the rather long homepage to view the contents list. Then you can simply click on the relevant county link for further resources. These include trade directories and almanacs, geographical and parish boundary information, church histories, indexes (and associated inscriptions), and transcribed historical documents.

www.abcounties.co.uk/newgaz/section1.htm
Gazetteer of British Place Names

★ ★ ★ ★ UK

Reliable and rapid, this is the easiest way to look up the location of even the smallest village.

www.historicaldirectories.org
Digital Library of Historical Directories

★ ★ ★ ★ UK

Leicester University is, with the help of some New Opportunities Funding, creating a digital library of 18th, 19th and 20th century directories, such as Kelly and Pigot. The lists of addresses and occupations such volumes contain can be vital material for genealogists, so this is a wonderful resource, especially as the search engine will highlight 'hits' for you in yellow. It will certainly become a five-star resource in the future.

www.villagesonline.com
Villages Online

★★★ UK

Villages Online is a portal with links to 800 village and community websites across the UK. You can search via the County or Alphabetical Listings. The historical data on offer is only as good as the individual websites, and it's fair to say that the process can be a bit hit and miss. If the locals are passionate about their village history though, you might find some gems. One website went so far as to list the villagers lost in wars through the ages. At the very least you'll be able to find a decent Bed and Breakfast, should you need to make a journey to continue your search in person.

www.balh.co.uk
British Association for Local History

★★★★ UK

This national charity publishes two magazines, *The Local Historian* and *Local History News*, and also issues the invaluable Local History Catalogue, an index of books on all aspects of local history. Don't miss the Useful Links, a substantial and highly relevant list of websites, including the Victoria Histories of the Counties of England. The Historical Association and (much further down the page) the increasingly useful Curious Fox UK Gazetteer. The Association also runs many interesting lectures and events.

www.local-history.co.uk
Local History Magazine

★★★★ UK

This site is mainly an online advertisement for Local History Magazine, but of particular interest is the list of local history societies. From this you can contact the relevant branch of the society. The onward links are also very helpful.

www.genuki.org.uk/Societies
Genuki

★★★★★ UK

One of the many useful pages tucked away on GENUKI. This list includes a number of genealogical and local history societies that are not members of the Federation of Family History Societies, and are not therefore listed on the FFHS site (see p.40).

London

http://booth.lse.ac.uk
Charles Booth Online Archive

Overall rating: ★ ★ ★ ★ ★			
Classification: Archive		**Readability:**	★ ★ ★ ★ ★
Updating: Regularly		**Content:**	★ ★ ★ ★ ★
Navigation: ★ ★ ★ ★ ★		**Speed:**	★ ★ ★ ★

(UK)

This is one of the most advanced and satisfying websites on the internet. Charles Booth's famous survey of Victorian London was published as 'Life and Labour in London 1886-1903'. For the online project, the vast archive of notebooks (compiled for the survey by Booth and his team) has been indexed and digitised. Booth conducted in-depth interviews with Londoners to understand the conditions in which they lived and worked, and the results provide extraordinary insight into what life must have been like for so many of our urban ancestors. As well as the narrative account of his findings, Booth produced a series of 'Maps Descriptive of London Poverty', with each street colour-coded to show the exact economic conditions, ranging from Black (Vicious, Semi-Criminal), Dark Blue (Chronic Want) through various shades of purple and pink, to Yellow (Wealthy). These maps are also available online in a highly interactive form.

SPECIAL FEATURES

Introduction and Guides to the Archives The obvious place to start to understand the riches of this site and the Booth archive of notebooks, held at the London School of Economics.

Poverty Maps of London Browse or Search This gives you two ways of accessing the poverty maps. Browse takes you to an overview of the map and you can zoom in on any part that takes your fancy. Search gives you the choice of entering current street names, postcodes or Wards, or landmarks or parishes from 1898. If you know the street where your ancestors lived, type it into the search box, and you will be taken straight to relevant part of Booth's map. From the colour key you can check the average socio-economic status of residents of that street at the end of the nineteenth century. The map can be compared with a modern map, allowing you to check whether the street still exists or has been demolished or renamed, and what the nearest tube stop would be if you are planning a visit. A pull-down menu showing 'From this page you can...' allows you to jump to other information in the archives relevant to that street or place.

Search the Catalogue of Original Survey Notebook Pages Type in a location, place of interest, occupation or keyword and you will see all the indexed references held within the archive. Many of the pages have been scanned and digitised and can be viewed online either as jpegs, or dDjvu (for which you need a special plug-in to view).

Inquiry into Life and Labour in London allows you to Browse the Police Notebooks, taking a street-by-street tour around London neighbourhoods, conducted by the remarks made by the police who escorted Booth's team of researchers. Absolutely fascinating social history. You can also explore themes such as childhood, crime, drink/drugs and smells. Under the last you will discover first-hand accounts of the distincitve mixture of glue and strawberry jam aromas that pervaded the streets of Bermondsey, while Newington suffered the from the smell of decaying fish.

Although genealogists are unlikely to find references to individual ancestors here unless they were directly involved in the project (the interviewees' names were changed to protect their identity), this amazing site provides unique background information.

http://collage.nhil.com
Corporation of London Library and Art Gallery Electronic

Overall rating: ★ ★ ★ ★ ★			
Classification:	Image Bank	**Readability:**	★ ★ ★ ★
Updating:	Occasionally	**Content:**	★ ★ ★ ★ ★
Navigation:	★ ★ ★ ★ ★	**Speed:**	★ ★ ★ ★

(UK)

www.corpoflondon.gov.uk/archives/lma
London Metropolitan Archives

Overall rating: ★ ★ ★ ★ ★			
Classification: Records		**Readability:**	★ ★ ★ ★
Updating:	Regularly	**Content:**	★ ★ ★ ★
Navigation:	★ ★ ★	**Speed:**	★ ★ ★ ★

(UK)

COLLAGE features an interactive database of the images in the Corporation of London's collection of paintings, drawing maps, engravings and photographs. The database contains over 20,000 works from the Guildhall Library (see p.47) and the Guildhall Gallery. Many of the images can be ordered online as prints, which can then be posted to you. The collection is particularly strong on London buildings, topography and people, but there is enough general historical material here to tempt people without connections to London. The site is brilliantly simple to use; the images are quick to download and can be enlarged by double-clicking. To find images that might be of relevance to your own search either use the search box, or browse by categories.

Search Tested with a single, admittedly unusual, surname known to have London associations, this produced three fascinating engravings that were absolutely relevant and previously unknown – a most rewarding result.

Browse Categories include Abstract Ideas, Archaeology and Architecture, History, Leisure, Military and War, Natural World, Politics, Religion and Belief, Society, Trade and Industry. More categories are listed further down the page.

Even if your ancestors were not distinguished enough to have their portraits featured in this collection, you are likely to find pictures of where they worshipped, played, courted or were educated. A great resource for enlivening a family tree.

Formerly the Greater London Records Office, the LMA houses an extraordinarily broad collection. It really is true to say that all of London life is here, from religion to the law, from schools to businesses, and from housing to hospitals. The photograph collection alone contains two million images. Many of the original parish registers from London churches are held here.

SPECIAL FEATURES

About LMA explains a little of what is contained in the collection's 31 miles of archives.

Our Collections will take you to the Galleries section, with a changing selection from LMA's collection of visual materials (the Anglo-Jewish collection seems a semi-permanent fixture). You can also follow a link to the European Visual Archive (EVA), a joint project that is putting many images from the collection online.

London Generations The most useful addition to this site since last reviewed, this is a database compiled from genealogical sources held at the LMA, so you can now check in advance if they hold the particular material you are looking for, and make a note of the call numbers. This means that if you are planning a visit you do not have to spend valuable research time at the archives searching for these. (Note: it can be helpful to know which modern London borough the location your target falls within when using the database).

Free LMA Leaflets leads to a growing list of downloadable fact sheets for which you will need Adobe Acrobat Reader, available on the spot (please refer to instructions on p.22).

Access and Enquiry Service gives details of the various ways of accessing the archive, and the knowledgeable team available to help you. Simple queries are answered for free, but for anything that requires consulting the records click on Family History Research Service. The services of the research staff are available for more complex searches at a rate of £24 per hour. You can now apply online or print an application form.

Relatively little is available for reading online here, but the online catalogue and research service are very welcome additions, and the downloadable leaflets are also worthwhile. If you are planning to visit the LMA, which is not far from the Family Records Centre (see p.43), then an online visit will help you to plan your research time to the full.

www.londonancestor.com
London Ancestor

Overall rating: ★ ★ ★ ★

Classification:	Transcripts	Readability:	★ ★ ★ ★
Updating:	Regularly	Content:	★ ★ ★ ★
Navigation:	★ ★ ★ ★	Speed:	★ ★ ★ ★

UK

London Ancestor describes itself as 'a web site of data for genealogy and local history in Greater London, containing extracts and transcripts from manuscripts, directories, ephemera and other difficult to find and out of print material, mostly pre-1880'. It is fabulously eclectic, and finding a missing ancestor on the site would be serendipitous rather than likely, but there is plenty here to educate and amuse. Site Map is probably the best way to explore the riches buried here, unless you know what you're looking for, in which case use the Search facility. However, you shouldn't miss the chance just to browse through the offerings.

SPECIAL FEATURES

There are too many special features to list here in detail but the following are some of the highlights:

Newspaper Extracts and Index provides details of inquests, accidents and incidents such as suicides and fires from 1830/31.

Metropolitan Police Daily Orders includes details of promotions, reprimands and commendations. Useful if you have a police ancestor around 1861.

Leigh's New Picture of London is an 1819 map of London and its environs. At 1mb it takes a while to download but it excellent at conveying a sense of how London's urban sprawl grew out of a series of small villages.

Views of London Churches, Buildings, Cityscapes from around 1830.

Kent's Directory for London Westminster and Southwark 1794.

London Ward and Parish maps from the eighteenth and nineteenth centuries.

Street Literature, found under Miscellaneous, covers contemporary reports of executions, politics and royalty and is only one of many fascinating items in this section.

Dictionary of Archaic Words helpfully lists definitions of some of the linguistic gems that slipped out of use.

Essential Links will also reward exploration, offering links to sites dealing with Lost London Streets, Public Houses, Historic Documents and much else besides.

A labour of love, and worth returning to regularly to see what fresh nuggets have been offered up.

www.steeljam.dircon.co.uk
Steeljam

Overall rating: ★ ★ ★ ★			
Classification:	Records	**Readability:**	★ ★ ★ ★
Updating:	Regularly	**Content:**	★ ★ ★ ★
Navigation:	★ ★ ★ ★	**Speed:**	★ ★ ★ ★

UK

Steve and Rita James, members of the London and North Middlesex FHS, maintain this exceptionally useful site that specialises primarily, though not exclusively, in London records. The site's usefulness is two-fold: first, it doesn't try to do too much – it concentrates specifically on London – and, second, it gives a great deal of carefully presented information about where London records are to be found and what you will find in them. Examples from the blue-lettered links on the homepage are: Churches in the City of London (many with photograph symbols alongside, which you click to enlarge; the way back is to minimise in the top right-hand corner of your browser toolbar), Lord Mayors of London and Parishes of Middlesex. Some links look further afield, for instance, the Index of County Record Offices.

SPECIAL FEATURES

A View of.... provides three articles introducing major London records centres, namely the Family Records Centre, The Guildhall Library and The London Metropolitan Archives. What is so valuable is that each gives an account of these centres from a user's point of view, literally explaining which way you turn as you walk in the main door. These accounts state what is easily found and where, what is less easily discovered, and also give such useful details as nearby restaurants or parks, and even where within the LMA you can buy pencils (which are obligatory if you are consulting their records)!

Parish Locator Software is a great little program that displays all the parishes within a specified number of miles from a known parish. Very useful for tracking down places your ancestors might have moved to, and suggesting which parish registers to check next. You can download DOS and Windows versions of the programe from the site (nothing for Mac users alas!). Gerry's home-page explains.

Excellent for tracking down and understanding London records – and if you are a 'virgin' researcher, the descriptions of what to expect at the three locations mentioned above are both helpful and reassuring.

Ireland

Included in this section are some sites that deal with the whole of Ireland, both north and south, particularly those that refer to pre-partition times. Sites referring specifically to Northern Ireland start on p.83.

It is also worth looking at apparently Scottish sites (such as www.scotlandclans.com) as they often have Irish records lumped in, particularly on American sites.

www.nationalarchives.ie
The National Archives of Ireland

Overall rating: ★ ★ ★ ★			
Classification: Records		**Readability:**	★ ★ ★ ★ ★
Updating: Regularly		**Content:**	★ ★ ★ ★ ★
Navigation: ★ ★ ★ ★		**Speed:**	★ ★ ★
IRE			

The homepage explains that relatively few of the archives can be consulted online. The object of the site is to explain what the archives contain and help you plan a visit.

SPECIAL FEATURES

About Us Start your exploration by clicking here, and then select About the National Archives: Some Facts. Next, clicking on Archives Held by the National Archives explains what does still exist, given that at the beginning of the Civil War in 1922 almost all the archives held by the Public Record Office of Ireland were destroyed by fire.

Genealogy leads to a page with further links to the various areas of the archival holdings. **Census Returns** (which includes 1901 and 1911 census returns and some remnants of returns from 1821, 1831, 1841 and 1851), micro-film copies and transcripts of some Church of Ireland registers. **Tithe Applotment** and **Primary (Griffith) Valuation, Wills and Testamentary Records** and **Births, Marriages and Deaths** are just some of the headings.

Other links include **Genealogy Centres Listed by County** and **Genealogical and Historical Researchers**.

From this list, Genealogy Links will be among the most useful, offering a list of further organisations which may be of help, including the IreAtlas Townland Database, an Irish Emigrants site, Records of the Irish Constabulary and of The Valuation Office of Ireland, and many others.

January 2003 saw the introduction of a New Genealogy Service, though this refers to what is available if you visit in person, not what can be accessed online.

This densely informative website is certainly a good starting point if you have Irish connections, as it has numerous onward links, although loading may be slow.

www.genuki.org.uk/big/irl
GENUKI Ireland

★★★★★ UK

In keeping with the tradition of the GENUKI resources, this is, without doubt, the place to start for an overview of both Irish genealogy and the most useful links available on the internet.

www.nli.ie
National Library of Ireland

★★★★ EI

Roman Catholic Parish registers of most parishes up to 1880 are held on microfilm. A Parish Registers list is available as a PDF. Their collections also include Estate Records, Gaelic Manuscripts, and a guide to family history in the library. Excellent Catalogues of Photographs and Prints and Drawings are available too; many items are viewable online.

www.ireland.com/ancestor
The Irish Times Online Irish Ancestors

★★★★ EI £ 🔒

Type in the name you are looking for, and this site will show you the distribution of mentions by county from a primary valuation property survey of 1848-64, an 1890 births distribution, and direct you to a surname dictionary, suggested variants, and details of placenames. A certain amount of information is available free but to get to a detailed level, such as to access to Lewis' Topgraphical Dictionary of Ireland (1837), you need to pay in dollars.

www.rootsweb.com/~irish/index.html
Irish Genealogical Society, International

★★★★★ US

The pages of the Irish Genealogical Society International, based in Minneapolis, include articles, guides, original sources and helpful tips. The most useful sections are Genealogy Information by IGSI and Irish Genealogy Links.

www.rootsweb.com/~fianna
Fianna

★★★★ US

Fianna is an Online Study Group for Irish Genealogy. Although it doesn't seem to have been updated recently, Fianna's archive highlights include the guide, which provides ideas and resources for anyone starting to research in Ireland, Transcriptions from Primary Sources and a comprehensive section on Irish Surnames, their variations and surname lists.

www.ifhf.org
The Irish Family History Forum

★★★ UK

Founded in 1991 by a small group of genealogical enthusiasts, the Forum is now incorporated in the US, and has connections in both Canada and England. It runs meetings, publishes a newsletter and will undertake research on behalf of individuals. **Links** is the most useful part of the site for UK genealogists.

www.scotlandsclans.com
Scotland's Clans

★★★ UK £

On the homepage scroll down to the link at the bottom for Irish Clans and Genealogy. This has interesting links to small sites featuring online transcriptions of Irish records, organised by county. Within this section there is a link to Irish Source Records, a subscription service that claims to have records of 190,000 Irish individuals, including reconstructions of census records that were lost in the 1922 fire. It costs $14.99 for a monthly subscription or you can purchase the database on CD-rom. As we haven't tried out this service, it's a case of caveat emptor. Other items of interest are the Message Boards, Surname pages, Cemetery Records, and Ships Passenger Lists (though these inevitably turn out to be for emigration to the US).

www.irishorigins.com
Irish Origins

★★★★ EI

This well-constructed, logically indexed site has a powerful search facility, hosted by Origins.net and covering both Northern Ireland and the Republic. Navigation is easy and exploration rewarding (and free).

www.from-ireland.net/index.htm
From Ireland

★★★★ EI

Jane Lyons maintains this useful website with particularly good explanations of how to make the most of the massive Rootsweb resource. See the For Newbies link.

www.irishroots.net
The Irish Family History Foundation

★★★ EI

The IFHF is the co-ordinating body of a network of genealogical research centres throughout Ireland. There is a centre for each county. The Foundation's website includes links to each centre and details of the services they provide.

www.igrsoc.org
The Irish Genealogical Research Society

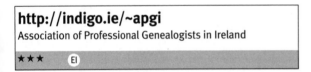
★ ★ ★   UK

The Society was established in London in 1936, where it has its own library. The site provides details of membership, activities and collections. There are plans for a members-only section where they will publish material from the library holdings online.

http://indigo.ie/~apgi
Association of Professional Genealogists in Ireland

★ ★ ★   EI

The site provides a list of members available to undertake paid research for you, as well as details of membership and links.

Northern Ireland

http://proni.nics.gov.uk
The Public Record Office of Northern Ireland

Overall rating: ★ ★ ★ ★			
Classification:	Irish records	Readability:	★ ★ ★ ★ ★
Updating:	Regularly	Content:	★ ★ ★ ★ ★
Navigation:	★ ★ ★ ★ ★	Speed:	★ ★ ★ ★

UK

As the homepage suggests, start with Questions, which clearly explains PRONI's role. It holds both central and local government records, and certain records belonging to private individuals. The records cannot be consulted online, but there is plenty of information to help you in advance to make the most of a visit to PRONI. Remember that many Irish records were burnt in Dublin in 1922.

SPECIAL FEATURES

The Records In Proni is a clear description of the records available.

Census Records, Church Records, Emigration Records, Poor Law Records and **School Records** are only a few of the records held. Further down the same page, those that are particularly relevant to tracing family history are listed again, followed by those relating to local history. Another link from this page leads to Academic Research and then to an interesting article on the Major Research Strengths of PRONI. Other links from the homepage include **Exhibitions and Events** and **What's New**.

This thoroughly user-friendly site will enable you to build up a good picture of what records are held. Anyone with Irish connections should find it valuable.

www.groni.gov.uk
The General Register Office of Northern Ireland

Overall rating: ★ ★ ★ ★			
Classification:	Irish records	**Readability:**	★ ★ ★ ★ ★
Updating:	Regularly	**Content:**	★ ★ ★ ★ ★
Navigation:	★ ★ ★ ★ ★	**Speed:**	★ ★ ★ ★

UK 🔒

GRONI is the main repository of civil registration records in Northern Ireland, since 1922. You will need x-shockwave flash plug-ins to access the site.

SPECIAL FEATURES

FAQs Start here for an overview of what you can obtain from GRONI.

Certificates Although the indexes are not online, you can now order BDM certificates online if you have enough biographical details or, better still, the registration details (note that the reference numbers from the LDS are not applicable). If you prefer you can download a form to post.

Historical Records Book online to search the indexes up to two weeks in advance, or arrange for an assisted search.

GRONI is one step ahead of its English and Welsh equivalent in offering online ordering of BDM certificates.

www.nireland.com/genealogy/index.html
NI Genealogy

★ ★ ★ ★   UK

This is about as unflashy as it is possible for a website to be, and none the worse for that.

http://www.nisra.gov.uk
Northern Ireland Statistics and Research Agency

★ ★ ★   UK

NISRA preforms an equivalent function for Northern Ireland as the ONS does for England and Wales, collating statistics and holding the original civil records of births, deaths, marriages and adoptions. Useful more for general population statistics than individual records.

www.linenhall.com
The Linen Hall Library

★ ★ ★   UK

You will need a Flash plug-in for this site, and even then it is slow to load. If you persevere you will discover the treasures in Belfast's oldest library, including its Irish and Local Studies collection and its Genealogy and Heraldry collection, which includes pedigrees of thousands of prominent families, transcriptions of some parish registers, passenger lists, Irish memorial records, and the 1796 Spinning Wheel Premium Entitlement Lists, which includes 60,000 names of people eligible to receive a free spinning wheel.

www.uhf.org.uk
Ulster Historical Foundation

★ ★ ★   UK

Established in 1956, access to most of the Foundation's services is membership-dependent (£17 annually) but for anyone with a serious interest in research within the Province this is almost certainly worthwhile.

Scotland

www.gro-scotland.gov.uk
General Register Office for Scotland

Overall rating: ★ ★ ★ ★ ★

Classification:	BDMs	Readability:	★ ★ ★ ★ ★
Updating:	Regularly	Content:	★ ★ ★ ★
Navigation:	★ ★ ★ ★ ★	Speed:	★ ★ ★ ★

UK

The General Register Office for Scotland has shown the rest of the UK government departments the way in establishing access to primary records online, through its partnership with Origins, a private company that has undertaken the digitisation of BDMs and census records for Scotland. Civil registration began in 1855. Launching the updated website in September 2002, Deputy Justice Minister, Richard Simpson, said: 'by the end of 2003, Scotland will probably have the most complete online genealogical information source in the world.'

SPECIAL FEATURES

Site Map is the best way of discovering the full scope of this website, much of which, naturally, is devoted to current records and statistics rather than historical ones.

About Gros is a good starting place, although it is tucked away at the bottom of the homepage.

Family Records Searching Historical Records leads to a lot of useful general links about Gros's services, including a list of parishes, an index of Parochial records available as a PDF download, and details of buying records on microfilm.

Scotland's People leads to a separate, internal website that is the official source for parish register, civil registration and census records. Access costs £6 for 30 'credits' in a 24-hour period. A Newsletter and Discussion Group are available here.

Birth/Death/Marriage Certificates describes the various ways that you can apply for certficiates less than 100 years old, and therefore not available on the Scottish Origins site.

Family historians are well catered for on this excellent public records site.

www.scotsorigins.com
Scots Origins

Overall rating: ★ ★ ★

Classification:	BDMs	Readability:	★ ★ ★ ★ ★
Updating:	Regularly	Content:	★ ★ ★ ★
Navigation:	★ ★ ★ ★ ★	Speed:	★ ★ ★ ★

UK R 🔒

Much depleted since the severing of its connection with GROS, Scots Origins has introduced a 'sighting service' for which you pay online to have transcribed records emailed (or posted) to you. The only free parts of the search are the IGI (free anyway) and a place name search, which does produce a reference code for use in Census records.

Discussion Group You can subscribe to have messages delivered by email or view on:

http://groups.yahoo.com/group/scots-origins

Scots Life provides background articles on subjects such as diverse as The Poor Law, Fishing, Hogmanay and Weaving, to which anyone may contribute.

www.nas.gov.uk
National Archives of Scotland

★★★★★ UK

Formerly known as the Scottish Record Office, NAS is the main archive for sources of the history of Scotland as a separate kingdom, from the 12th century. It is a useful repository of public and legal records as well as of many local and private archives. This is an elegant and simple website , though restricting it to a two-thirds page width has made print rather small.

The Collections offers several categories, found from the Select menu.

Services to Researchers gives access to PDF files on subjects such as fees and changes. Under Researching Remotely it sets out clearly what they can and cannot help you with. The former includes making copies of documents, so if you have a very specific request, you may be in luck even if you can't visit the archives yourself.

Family History includes useful information about planning a visit to the archives in person, and a Family History FAQ that provides Fact Sheets on a wide range of topics from Adoption to Sassines, wills and inventories, which can be downloaded as PDF files.

www.nls.uk
National Library of Scotland

★★★★★ UK

The site has online catalogues of most of its holdings, and Digital Libary leads you to the selection of resources that can be consulted online, including an excellent selection of old maps.

www.genuki.org.uk/big/sct/
GENUKI Scotland

★★★★★ UK

This is the main index page for Scottish pages contained in the GENUKI site. Listings are arranged by county, and then thematically.

www.scan.org.uk
Scottish Archive Network

★★★★★ UK

Scan has the aim of providing internet access to the written history of Scotland, and the Online Catalogues are a finding aid for material in over 20,000 collections held by almost 50 separate Scottish archives. Family History gives a good introduction to tracing Scottish ancestors. There are also some good tips on deciphering Scottish handwriting.

www.scotlandsclans.com
Scotland's Clans

★★★★ UK

Much of the information here is either predictable links to other sites such as Ancestry.com, or gateways to paid sites, but if you click on Genealogy you'll find a more interesting set of links including ones to sites posting Scottish cemetery records, clans and family homepages, Scottish census records, message boards, passenger lists, and a page that helps you work out if your surnames are claimed by septs or clans (see Your Scottish Kin). There are also some pages and links of Irish interest.

www.sctbdm.com
Scotland BDM Exchange

★★★★ UK

The Scottish Birth Death Marriage Exchange, where you can post details of your own family, see what others have posted, perhaps saving you the cost of ordering a certificate, and make contact with other researching the same names. Over 10,000 records are listed.

www.drawn-evidence.dundee.ac.uk
The Drawn Evidence

★★★★ UK

A virtual archive of Scottish architectural plans and drawings, hosted by Dundee University. All images can be viewed online.

www.scottish-communities.net
Scottish Communities Web Database

★★★★ UK

A useful set of links to individual community sites for Scottish villages, towns, cities and areas.

www.ancestralscotland.com
Ancestral Scotland

★★★ UK

This site is aimed at tourists visiting Scotland to find their ancestors. It provides a good, simple introduction to researching Scottish family history, and provides a name, place and parish search box, drawing on data from the 1881 census for Scotland.

www.scottishdocuments.com
Scottish Documents

★★★ UK

Scottish Documents has an index of half a million testaments (wills) which you can order copies of online.

Wales

Official Welsh records are mostly covered on the main UK sites, such as the PRO, the FRC and ONS in chapter 2.

www.llgc.org.uk
The National Library of Wales

★★★★★ UK

As you'd expect, this site contains background information for readers and visitors to the National Library. **Family History** gives a brief introduction to their genealogical holdings, and provides a link to their Search Service, with a research request form for paid searches, which are available at £10 per hour. **Catalogues and Online Resources** includes a searchable database of over one and half million titles added since 1986. Of most interest to family historians, though, is the Marriage Bonds archive to be found within the ISYS:web (Minor Databases) section, for which you need to scroll down the page. In this archive you'll find an index of applicants for marriage licences from 1616 to 1837. A great resource, and for once, it's free!

http://genuki.org.uk/big/wal
GENUKI Wales

★★★★★ UK

Once again, GENUKI provides the most detailed set of links to sites covering guides to Welsh genealogy, church records, look-up exchanges, surname lists, a guide to patronymic naming, plus local and family history sites.

http://home.clara.net/tirbach.LEWales.html
All Wales Look-Up Exchange

★★★★ UK

A wide range of books, research aids and directories are listed for free look-ups by volunteers.

www.brawdybooks.com
Brawdy Books

★★★★ UK

Major Francis Jones, the late Wales Herald at Arms, assembled a great deal of information about Welsh ancestry, and also wrote numerous articles. This material is now made available from this website. You can access maps of all the parishes by county, indexes of the main families and houses that appear in his works (available to purchase online) which cover Camarthenshire and Pembrokeshire and Cardiganshire. Research Services start at £25, then £15 per hour including costs.

www.celtic-connect.demon.co.uk
Celtic Connect

★★★★ UK

Two graduates of the University of Wales started this enterprise, based in Aberystwyth, home of the National Library of Wales. They will undertake research at £15 per hour and provide a preliminary feasibility study before you commit to any payments.

www.lllgc.org.uk/cac
Archives Council Wales

★★★★ UK

Archives Council Wales provides links to all the archive repositories in Wales, including county records offices.

www.rootsweb.com/~wlsafhs
Association of Family History Societies of Wales

★★★★ UK

A simple web presence offering contact details for the relevant societies, and a decent set of Relative Links on research in Wales.

Other British Isles

http://user.itl.net/~glen/genukici.html
The Channel Islands Page

★★★★★ UK

Despite the atypical URL, this is the main GENUKI gateway page for Channel Islands Research, and part of Alex Glendinning's personal site.

www.rootsweb.com/~jfuller/ci.html
Channel Islands Genealogy

★★★★★ UK

Maintained by John Fuller, these pages provide access to a Channel Islands mailing list, Surname Interest List, Look-ups, index to an 1849 map of Jersey and some useful links.

http://user.itl.net/~glen/AbouttheChannelIslands.FHS.html
Channel Islands Family History Society

★★★★ UK

This is the best way in to a number of Channel Islands records, such as those held by the Société Jersiaise and the Société Guernsiaise (the latter has a very useful Family History section). See FAQs for a good list of onward links.

http://genealogy.about/com/es/channelislands
Channel Islands Genealogy and Family History

★★★ UK

It can be irritating when search engines repeatedly feed one into About.com but sometimes this massive directory comes up with the goods, as it does here.

www.isle-of-man.com
Isle of Man

★★★★★ UK

Hosts a map of IoM parishes, a database of researches, gedcom files, look-up exchange, bulletin board, an article about wills and other very useful links, and the pages of the IoM Family History Society. These links are found from Genealogy in the left-of-page index but have to be selected individually to open.

www.genuki.org.uk/big/iom
The URL for the Genuki Isle of Man contents.

Chapter 5

international & ethnic resources

There are websites on the internet that offer links to specific record-holding bodies in countries all over the world, or at any rate to those with websites. This chapter cannot possibly list them all, so what is offered here is a selection of those likely to be of most relevance to UK researchers.

Listing by star-rating order, which is the style followed in all the other chapters, would be nonsense here, so I have had to make an admittedly rather arbitrary decision about which national records are likely to be most useful to British users.

After the section of sites dealing with many different parts of the world come those records associated with other particular countries or ethnic groups, again listed in alphabetical, rather than star-rating, order. The categories are, of necessity, fairly arbitrary: some sites listed cover several nationalities, whilst other countries or ethnic groups are not listed at all. If the category in which you are interested does not have its own entry here, you will need to search another website, such as The Genealogy Home Page (see p.108), which has a link to World-Wide Genealogy Resources, or Cyndi's List (see p.33).

International

www.genealogylinks.net
Genealogylinks.net

Overall rating: ★ ★ ★ ★ ★			
Classification:	Records	**Readability:**	★ ★ ★ ★
Updating:	Regularly	**Content:**	★ ★ ★ ★
Navigation:	★ ★	**Speed:**	★ ★

US

This index of genealogy sites is very clearly catalogued, which makes using it a pleasure. On the homepage are two contents lists, the one on the left indicating what is in the databases, under All UK & Ireland, England, Scotland, Wales and Isle of Man, Europe, United States, Canada, Australia & NZ and Global Databases. The contents list on the right offers What's New, Top 22 Genealogy Sites, plus some teasers for paid-for sites such as the ubiquitous Ancestry.com and Genealogy.com.

SPECIAL FEATURES

Cemeteries, Censuses, Military and **Ships, Passenger Lists (in Global Databases)** Apart from a few general entries at the beginning of each, the various national sections are also subdivided into these categories, although there are not necessarily any links in every one of the categories for every country.

United States Clicking here, however, you will find that the lists are far more complete, with Canada and Australia & NZ not far behind.

A good gateway site to many countries.

www.worldgenweb.org
The WorldGenWeb Project

Overall rating: ★ ★ ★ ★			
Classification:	Records	**Readability:**	★ ★ ★
Updating:	Occasionally	**Content:**	★ ★
Navigation:	★ ★ ★	**Speed:**	★ ★

INT

This is a volunteer-run organisation, launched in 1996, whose mission is to deliver genealogical information free of charge to researchers all over the world. Now hosted by RootsWeb (see p.30), each country's databank should be staffed by people who either live in or are familiar with that country's research resources. The result is only as good as the volunteers who contribute, and that, for the time being, is the problem. However, this site has made tremendous strides since the last edition, and deserves further support. Click on a region of the world map to see which countries are listed.

SPECIAL FEATURES

Europe is organised into British IslesGenWeb, CenEuroGenWeb, EastEuroGenWeb, and Mediterranean GenWeb, each of which is offered in several different languages – just click on a flag to view the appropriate version.

CaribbeanGenWeb Archives Is particularly well covered, and here you'll find a worthwhile list of records, such as the emigration lists for Bermuda or Jamaica, baptismal records in Antigua, or records of the Wesleyan Methodist Church or the Society of Friends (Quakers) in the British Virgin Islands. Alternatively, go in via Country Index, offered in Resources on the hompage.

This is one to watch for the future in the hope that it will eventually build into something really valuable.

African and Caribbean

www.channel4.com/untold
Channel 4 Untold - Black History Season

Overall rating: ★ ★ ★ ★ ★			
Classification:	Records	Readability:	★ ★ ★ ★
Updating:	Occasionally	Content:	★ ★ ★ ★
Navigation:	★ ★ ★ ★ ★	Speed:	★ ★ ★

UK

Television company websites can be infuriating for their propensity to clear out or move excellent back-up material after the programmes they are tied to have been broadcast. Untold has survived since 2000, and if enough people use it perhaps it will become a permanent fixture on Channel 4's site. As such, it is one of the best introductions to black history and genealogy on the web. The left-hand menu links to specific programme information from the Untold season of programmes. Putting the word Genealogy into the search box will produce details about an Extraordinary Ancestors series which should ensure more specific information. Below that, the drop-down menu in Subject Search offers various options, including Diaspora, Family History and Immigration.

There is some excellent information here as long as it stays put.

www.bbc.co.uk/history/your_history/index.shtml
BBC Caribbean Family History

Overall rating: ★ ★ ★ ★			
Classification:	Records	Readability:	★ ★ ★
Updating:	Occasionally	Content:	★ ★ ★
Navigation:	★ ★ ★	Speed:	★ ★ ★ ★

UK

Click where it says 'discover your African Caribbean roots' to find a good overview of the problems and opportunities of researching Caribbean ancestors by Kathy Chater.

SPECIAL FEATURES

Wayne Younge's Story is a first-hand account of one man's search for his roots in Barbados.

African Roots traces the history of the slave trade and waves of settlement in the Caribbean and the effects of these on the records available.

Caribbean Family Records discusses the range of records available both in the islands of the West Indies, and in UK records offices such as the PRO and FRC.

Records before 1838 looks at the record sources dating back before the abolition of slavery, most of which relate to the estate owners, but some contain lists of slaves.

Go Further contains links and further reading.

The treatment is rather brief, but this is a good introduction to tracing Carribbean ancestors.

West Indies

www.candoo.com/surnames
Caribbean Surnames Index

★★★★ US

The West Indies Surname Interests List compiled by Vaughn W. Royal in Virginia, and reviewed in an earlier edition, is no longer accessible from a website. This site, therefore, is a another means of putting in touch those who are already researching individual West Indies surnames with those seeking information. Names are listed alphabetically island by island.

www.rootsweb.com/~caribgw
Caribbean GenWeb Project

★★★★ US

Each of the Islands has a website listing the resources available, which can be accessed from the homepage here under Island Links. Other resources to be found here are archives, mailings lists, queries, and research tips. There is a board for General Queries, if you don't know which Island your ancestor was from.

www.rootsweb.com/~jamwgw
Genealogy of Jamaica

★★★★★ US

The church and civil records of Jamaica are better preserved than those for many other islands, and the genealogical community better established, so this is a rewarding place from which to explore genealogy in Jamaica, as it includes, maps, articles, historical background, links and primary records, including manumission of slaves transcribed from files at the PRO. There is a link to AfriGeneas (see below).

www.jamaicanfamilysearch.com
Jamaican Family Search

★★★★ US R 🔒

A wonderful collection of transcriptions from a huge variety of sources covering over 130,00 individuals. The records cover wills, advertisements, manumissions and church records. Some pages are free to access, and others are members only and require a fee, starting $4 for a week's consultation, and payment is by secure server. You can earn a free subscription by contributing records to the site. At the very bottom of the very long homepage, you'll find a search box where you can search for specific names across all the lists. Inevitably the majority link to US-based information.

Africa

www.rootsweb.com/~africagw
Africa GenWeb Project

★★★★ US

Each of the African countries has a website here, though as yet many are in need of volunteer coordinators. The only countries with significant information online are Côte d'Ivoire, Ghana, Namibia, Nigeria, South Africa and Zimbabwe, though this is likely to improve. There is a link to AfriGeneas (see below).

www.afrigeneas.com
AfriGeneas

★★★★ US R

A slick site dealing predominantly with African-American heritage, though dedicated to providing resources for people tracing ancestors throughout the diaspora. The Slave Data Collection draws on an impressive range of sources, and can be browsed by surname or state. The site also carries census data, surname lists, a library of articles and records, and a comprehensive set of links about black history and genealogy. Inevitably, the majority is US-based information.

Asia

See also India p.105.

www.rootsweb.com/~asiagw
Asia GenWeb Project

★★★★ US

As with other parts of the GenWeb project, some countries are much better represented than others, reflecting the level of official records, internet penetration and interest in genealogy in the countries themselves and among the emigrant communities, but this is likely to be as good a starting point as any for most Asian countries.

http://user.itl.net/~glen/asianintro.html
Alex Glendinning's Asian Pages

★★★★ US

This site concentrates on British subjects and prisoners of war in Asia, particularly Singapore and Malaya, with links to other sites of Asian interest, and a list of Asian researchers.

www.casbah.ac.uk
Casbah

★★★ UK

Hosted by the University of London Computer Centre, Casbah is a joint development between the Institute of Commonwealth Studies and the PRO to develop an online resource for Caribbean and Black and Asian studies. At the moment only a sample is available, but keep an eye on this one.

Australasia

www.cohsoft.com.au/afhc
The Australian Family History Compendium

Overall rating: ★ ★ ★ ★ ★			
Classification:	Records	Readability:	★ ★ ★ ★ ★
Updating:	Regularly	Content:	★ ★ ★ ★
Navigation:	★ ★ ★ ★ ★	Speed:	★ ★ ★ ★ ★

AUS

This well-organised and rapid website is devoted to the exploration of Australian records, along with much other information about how to set about genealogical research, both in Australia and elsewhere.

SPECIAL FEATURES

The homepage is clearly set out under such headings as Beginners; Courses; Demographics and Population; Heraldry; Surname Searches; History, and so on.

AFHC Guide This comes near the top of the homepage, and is a link to the list of actual records that are available online. Each of these has its own link.

Where to find archives, libraries, and other repositories Further scrolling down the homepage brings you to this section with each of the states and territories listed. Click on the area of interest for comprehensive information about the regional resources to help your research, such as where to apply for BDM certificates.

This clear, general-purpose website is probably the best entry point for anyone seeking information about ancestors in Australia.

www.aigs.org.au
Australian Institute of Genealogical Studies Inc.

Overall rating: ★ ★ ★ ★			
Classification:	Records	Readability:	★ ★ ★ ★
Updating:	Regularly	Content:	★ ★ ★
Navigation:	★ ★ ★	Speed:	★ ★ ★ ★

AUS

This well-laid-out website is almost unobtrusive in its presentation. It proves to be a mine of information about Australian and associated records. The Institute also sells vouchers to access the British 1901 census.

SPECIAL FEATURES

The brown links on the homepage offer such categories as Library, Catalogue, Research Services, The Genealogist's Journal and Bookshop, all of which are self-explanatory.

Links, found from the News drop-down menu, contains some very useful material, including some searchable indexes. Many of these links go on to other websites, mostly Australian in origin. Those links tested were working well and the onward material on offer was impressive.

A valuable website for anyone exploring Australian connections, particularly those interested in searching the convict transportation records.

www.prov.vic.gov.au
Public Record Office - Victoria's Archives

★★★★ AU

The Public Records Office of Victoria is committed to putting many of its records online. From the homepage click on Access to the Collection for a straighforward database listing immigrants arriving at the Australian port of Victoria in 1852–1889, from British and foreign ports. For a Probate database follow the link to Archives@Victoria. This website was still under construction at the time of writing so its usefulness is difficult to evaluate. Further records are being added and indexed all the time.

The more information you give, the more likely you are to find the relevant match, but too much detail can also work against you, as the lists contain many entries without a forename, with passengers listed simply as Mr, Mrs or Infant, so do try all possible combinations. The homepage explains how to fill in the search boxes. A successful search will lead to a fiche number and page number, which can then be ordered.

This is a useful point from which to track down an emigrant to Australia, known to have landed in Victoria.

www.firstfamilies2001.net.au
First Families 2001

★★★★ AU

Funded by the Victoria Government, this project invited people to submit the details of their ancestors and stories about their lives. Although the project is now closed, you can search by surname to find possible connections, browse and make contact with any of the contributors. A very worthwhile site.

www.bdm.nsw.gov.au/bdmaus
Births, Deaths and Marriages Registries of Australasia

★★★★ AU

The full URL gives you quick links to the BDM registries for each part of Australasia. Leave off the final /bdmaus (from the URL given above) to be taken to the New South Wales BDM indexes which you can search online, along with a Wills Register.

http://users.bigpond.net.au/convicts
Claim-A-Convict

★★★★ AU

An index of over 20,000 convicts arriving from 1788 onwards compiled by Leslie Uebel. Further records are offered for sale on CD roms, plus lists of convicts' partners (many were never married) and a mailing list for people trying to trace deported ancestors.

www.macbeth.com.au
Macbeth Genealogical Services

★★★ AU

The links are in the top of the toolbar, both to Free Indexes and Macbeth's own products and services. They may not be cheap but if they save you the cost of a trip to Australia who's complaining?

http://home.vicnet.net.au/~shghs
Swan Hill Genealogical and Historical Society Inc

★★★★   AU

Clearly Swan Hill is an active and industrious Genealogical society based in Victoria. The Links section is indeed comprehensive and 'eclectic'. Particularly strong on family history societies, maps and gazetteers.

www.penrithcity.nsw.gov.au/loz/lozaust.htm
Lorraine's Top family History Internet Sites

★★★★   AU

Lorraine Stacker's well-maintained set of links to Australian sites is arranged by topic, covering categories such as Indigenous (Aboriginal) Family History, Cemeteries, Military History, newspapers and Researchers in Australia.

www.pcug.org.au/~pdownes
Patricia Downes' Genealogy Pages

★★★★   AU

The site provides indexes of convicts shipped to Australia with the First, Second and Third Fleets, and Irish convicts from 1791-1820.

Canada

www.archives.ca
Library and Archives of Canada

Overall rating: ★★★★			
Classification:	Records	Readability:	★★★
Updating:	Occasionally	Content:	★★★★
Navigation:	★★★	Speed:	★★★

CAN

From the landing page, click on either the word English or French in very small letters underneath the main logo, to read the site in either language. From the menu on the left of the page that you arrive at, the most pertinent sections are listed under Research.

SPECIAL FEATURES

Genealogy is the best place to start if you don't know what type of records are available as it gives an overview of searching for Canadian ancestors.

Archivia Net:Online Research Tool allows you to search the collections by theme or type of documents. The Finding Aids describe groups of documents or individual items, some of which are available online.

Services includes details of how to hire a freelance researcher or send a simple inquiry direct to the archives staff.

Publications (top of page) leads to a list that includes Tracing your Ancestors in Canada, a publication that can either be ordered online or downloaded as a PDF file.

Good information about Canadian records is certainly stored here, though it is not the easiest of websites to navigate.

www.islandnet.com/~jveinot/cghl/cghl.html
Canadian Genealogy and History

★★★★   CAN

If you have trouble loading this site from the URL given above, go to www.islandnet.com, click on the Members Pages icon, and type jveinot into the search box. You will be rewarded with an excellent set of links for Canadian family history arranged nationally, by province and by classification. If you are a regular visitor you have the option of viewing just the new listings made within the past 14 days.

www.rootsweb.com/~canwgw
Canada GenWeb Project

★★★★   CAN

Each of the Canadian provinces and territories has its own coordinator and set of pages, providing links and introductory information as well as actual records contributed by members.

http://freepages.genealogy.rootsweb.com/~britishhome children
The British Home Children

★★★★   CAN

A website devoted to helping reunite families broken up by the British Child Emigration Scheme to Canada, which was operative from 1870 to 1948. The very moving introduction explains the background, and there is a surname list of over 19,000 names of children affected. See also p. 117.

http://ist.uwaterloo.ca/~marj/genealogy/thevoyage.html
Immigrants to Canada

★★★★   CAN 🔒

An extraordinary range of material is collected here, including passenger lists and background information, such as emigrants' handbooks and personal accounts. Look under the Genealogy link too.

www.inGeneas.com
inGeneas

★★★   CAN

Set up by professional genealogists working in Ottawa, the inGeneas site provides indexes to passenger lists and other immigration documents, marriage and census records in a free online database, and you can use the online ordering facility to purchase a transcription of the full record of anything you find. The Resources Directory has a useful set of links. Research services are no longer offered.

Europe

The enthusiasm for genealogy online has not yet caught on to the same degree outside the anglophone countries, so this remains a patchy section. We've confined ourselves largely to sites that are presented in English, or offer such a useful resource that they cannot be overlooked. Don't forget to check the sites in the general International section at the beginning of the chapter, particularly WorldGenWeb, or the country listings in Cyndi's list (p.33). Rootsweb (p. 30) will have mailing lists and surname boards for almost every nationality you care to mention. Also there are many American groups that celebrate their European roots, and a quick search on Google with 'genealogy' or 'family history' and the name of the country you are interested in should produce some promising leads.

Eastern and Central Europe

www.eegsociety.org
East European Genealogical Society

★★★   US

If all you know is a surname or the name of a village, this would probably be the best place to start trying to find out more about your East European connections. Read the homepage first and then move on to the Database Search of the Surname/Village Index. Back Issues links to the Journal of the Society of Eastern European Genealogists.

www.feefhs.org
Federation of East European Family History Societies

★★★   US

Despite the name, this site covers central Europe (Austria, Germany, Switzerland) as well as Eastern Europe and Russia. Distinctly low-tech in feel, the site nonetheless pulls together plenty of resources, including a Map Room, email newsletter and a genealogy tool kit. Either use the Ethnic, Religious and National Index to find your way to what you need, or use the FEEFHS Website (Web Portal) Index to perform a search. As the site covers material from a very wide range of countries and languages, transliteration can be an issue, and as there is no Soundex facility, you may need to try variant spellings in your searches.

France

www.francogene.com
FrancoGene

★★★★ CAN

The emphasis here is on French immigration to the US and Canada, but under The Ancient World you'll find a good set of resources for searching in France, as well as Belgium, Switzerland and Italy, for French ancestors. Use the site map (in Tools) to uncover the depths of the site, and it is worth scrolling down to the regional listings, or you can use the search box on the homepage if you know what you're looking for. Most of the site is in English except where it refers you to pages from www.genealogie.com, the francophone version of the site.

www.geneaguide.com
GeneaGuide

★★★★ · FR

When you reach the homepage of this French genealogical portal, click on the little Union Jack flag to view the English version. You'll find a list of the articles available in the menu on the left-hand side, with information on specific provinces in France. www.geneaguide.com/anglais/civil.htm takes you directly to an extremely useful article by Patrick Pontet of the Anglo-French Family History Society (more details of which are found on this site) introducing the civil registration process in France, plus a lot of cultural background information, from French handwriting to what happens to women's surnames at different stages of their lives, to help you interpret your findings.

Huguenots

www.huguenot.net
Huguenot

★★★★ CAN

A portal for English-speaking descendants of the French Protestant refugees in the sixteenth and seventeenth centuries, with good links to sites on Huguenot history and genealogy, as well as a message board.

www.island.net/~andreav/
Huguenots-Walloons-Europe Mailing List

★★★★ CAN

Here you'll find an introduction to the RootsWeb sponsored genealogy mailing list for Huguenots-Walloons-Europe. Beyond the Basics leads to a message board, surname list, a Huguenot/Walloon History and Timeline and links to many other sites of related interest.

www.ucl.ac.uk/library/huguenot.htm
The Huguenot Library

★★★ UK

You'll find details of how to access this important collection of books, manuscripts, prints and engravings, as well as a good list of publications and information sources, and links to relevant societies, including www.huguenotsociety.org.uk. This was still under construction at the time of review but would be worth consulting in future.

Germany

www.rootsweb.com/~wggerman
Germany GenWeb Project

★★★★ US

This part of the CenEuroGenWeb project has won awards for the quality of its resources, including maps, ships lists and a good section about civil registration in Germany (though the map is slow to download). There is a separate section for Prussia.

http://home.bawue.de/~hanacek/info/edatbase.htm
Internet Sources of German Genealogy

★★★★ DE

Andreas Hanacek provides a well-organised list of links for tracing German ancestors, which is particularly strong on regional resources, and includes sources outside Germany (Austria, Switzerland, Poland) where these are relevant.

www.genealogienetz.de
Det Deutsche Genealogie Server

★★★★ DE

There is an English language version of this portal in which many web-pages of relevance to German researchers can be found. Austria, Switzerland and other German-speaking countries are also covered.

www.germanroots.com
German Roots

★★★ US

You will find a good set of links here, plus a very useful Basic Research Outline for German Genealogy, suitable for beginners and intermediate researchers, and a collection of emigration and immigration resources, such as passenger lists, naturalizations, though the emphasis is naturally on emigration to the US.

Italy

http://gens.labo.net
Gens

★★★★ IT

This site breaks our rule about only listing English-language websites, because the surname distribution feature here is so brilliant and simple to use. Type the Italian surname you want to research into the top search box on the left under the word Cognome. You will then see a map of Italy showing the distribution of that surname through the regions. Click on any of the regions to see a larger-scale map showing the areas of concentration within that region. Gens also offers a dictionary of Italian names, background on each of the regions, a newsletter and genealogical research.

www.rootsweb.com/~itawgw
Italy World GenWeb

★★★★　US

The place to start for an introduction to tracing Italian roots and further links, surname boards and passenger lists, though there are precious few records online. Those that are available are in Archives, 'Records that we have online contributed by our fantastic friends'.

http://italiangenealogy.tardio.com/html
The Italian Genealogy Homepage

★★★　IT

A set of facinating articles on issues concerning genealogical research and its difficulties in Italy. Some of the same information, but also some additional material is available at www.regalis.com/italgen.htm

www.daddezio.com
Italian Genealogy

★★★　IT

Illya James D'Addezio has created this lively, articulate website for those researching Italian connections.

Netherlands

www.cbg.nl/english/englishpag.htm
Centraal Bureau voor Genealogie

★★★★　NL

This is the principal website for tracing Dutch connections, and it also gives access to the collections of the Royal Dutch Society for Genealogy and Heraldry. **Online Research Guide** leads to a further link, entitled How to Start Searching for Dutch Ancestors, a clear and helpful article that can be read online. Other possibly useful titles are **Primary Genealogical Records in the Netherlands** and **Heraldry**. **Links** transports you to a long, well-organised list of further websites you may wish to consult. Those tested were working well, although the headings are in Dutch.

www.dotukdirectory.co.uk/global/Europe/Netherlands/Society_and_Culture/Genealogy

★★★　NL

Kees Klootwijk's list of links may move at any moment to be hosted elsewhere, so if this database of Netherland's websites disappears try his name in www.google.co.uk (selecting 'pages from the UK' option).

Romany and Travellers

http://website.lineone.net/~rtfhs
Romany & Traveller Family History Society

★★★★ UK

This straightforward site is the place to come if you have Romany, traveller or gypsy connections. **Was your Ancestor a Gypsy?** is a good general introduction to the subject. **Publications** contains a detailed list of books and transcriptions. **Romany Routes** is the Society's Journal. Clicking here leads to indexes of the surnames that appear in each of the recent issues, as well as a list of members' interests. There's also a useful list of other websites from which to explore the history of the Romany lifestyle.

http://sca.lib.liv.ac.uk/collections/gypsy/intro.htm
Gypsy Collections at the University of Liverpool

★★★★ UK

As well as details of the collection held at the library, on the site you will find bibliographies, photographs, links and details of other gypsy collections.

Scandinavia

http://digitalarkivet.uib.no
National Archives of Norway

★★★★★ NO

Well, Norway has certainly got its act together! The National censuses for 1801, 1865 and 1900 are all searchable online, along with tax lists, military rolls, church registers, emigrants, probate registers, fire assessment registers and citizenship papers. They are not all complete but this is nonetheless a very ambitious undertaking, simply but effectively executed, and it's free! It is also available in English by clicking when you reach the homepage.

www-personal.umich.edu/~cgaunt/scandinavia.html
Scandinavian Genealogy Resources on the Internet

★★★★ US

Chris Gaunt's set of links cover all of Scandinavia, and at the bottom of the page there you can click through to lists specific to Norway and Sweden, and mailing lists for Denmark and Finland as well as Norway and Sweden.

www.dis.se/denindex.htm
DIS Computer Genealogy Society of Sweden

★★★★ SW

This well-established group's site is available in English from the URL given above. You can search the DISBYT databases of submitted GEDCOM files, which also cover Germany, Finland and Norway as well as Sweden.

http://geocities.com/familysk/research.html
Slovak Genealogy Assistance

★★★

Stefan Eonka offers research help for those with Slovakian connections. Fees are reasonable.

Spain

www.ldelpino.com/geneal.html
Spanish Genealogy

★★★★ ES

This offers Tips & Techniques, Useful Resources, Towns & Parishes and Archives, among many further possibilities. Almost everything here is available in English as well as Spanish.

General

http://uk.dir.yahoo.com/arts/humanities/history/genealogy/regional_and_ethnic_resources/
Yahoo Directory

★★★

This page within the Yahoo directory gives access to further possibilities, such as Belgium, Poland, Russia and Switzerland, as well as other countries outside Europe.

India

www.ozemail.com.au/~clday
Family History in India

★★★★★ AU

Cathy Day has produced a great resource for people tracing British, European and Anglo-Indian family history in India Burma, Pakistan and Bangladesh. A simple search facility allows you to scan the names of over 60,000 families, locations, regiments and occupations relating to the colonial period. Starting Out provides an introduction to tracing ancestors in British India. The site also gives introductions to and extracts from church records, cemetery records, and other sources, as well as copious background information and photographs. Without doubt, this is the place to start.

www.bl.uk/collections/orientaloffice.html
India Office Library

★★★★ UK

The British Library houses the India Office Records of pre-1947 government of India, and these pages explain what is contained in the collection. Click on Sources for Family History Research for an introduction to the library's holdings. Descendants of East India company employees, Indian Civil Service and Indian Army Personnel will find these particularly rewarding. The records are not available to consult online, but for background information and to prepare to visit the library this site is invaluable.

www.indiaman.com
The Indiaman Magazine

★★★★ UK

This magazine is aimed at helping family historians trace records of ancestors of British and European origin in India and South East Asia from 1600 to the twentieth century. Whether or not you choose to subscribe to the magazine, the list of web links is very worthwhile, and for a nominal fee you can add your name to the Indiaman Genealogical Register.

www.movinghere.org.uk/galleries/roots/sasian/sasian.htm
South Asian Roots
★★★ (UK)

This is part of a larger website, Moving Here, that contains much good historical material about some of Britain's ethnic communities and the reasons that brought them here. (It also covers Caribbean, Irish and Jewish immigrants). The South Asian pages are rich in detail, often very poignant and contain features on Tracing South Asian Roots and Anglo-Indians.

Jewish

www.jgsgb.org.uk
Jewish Genealogical Society of Great Britian
★★★★★ (UK)

Trying to find Jewish connections is greatly helped by coming here first. Among the valuable records available online for consultation is **The JGSGB Index of Marriages**, recorded at the Princelet (Princes) Street Synagogue in Spitalfields, London, from 1897–1907. It can be viewed via the bride's or the bridegroom's surname. The real depth of this website is reavealed by opening the Useful Links page, found at the bottom of the Resources & Databases menu.

Cemetery Records Index Page is another recently completed page, allowing search by surname of the burials at the two Jewish cemeteries at Cheshunt and Enfield.

JGSGB Family Finder leads to a search service that can either be downloaded in its entirety or, if you are a member, be accessed via email. There is much else here besides.

www.hum.huji.ac.il/dinur
The Jewish History Resource Center
★★★★★ (IS)

A thorough and well-maintained set of international links, with particularly good coverage of Sephardic genealogy. Each of the headings below the central logo has a drop-down menu found by clicking on the down-facing arrow.

www.jewishgen.org
JewishGen
★★★★ (US) (R)

Though the US origins of this site are very clear, it works hard to provide world coverage and there is plenty of relevance to the UK researcher including the London Jews Database (1790-1850). The very active discussion group is a great resource, and the Family Finder lists over 200,000 surnames and towns being researched. Obviously you should also look under the country of origin of your ancestors, and try the Shtetl Links section. Start by selecting Databases from the Research List on the homepage and then move around by country.

www.jeffreymaynard.com
Anglo-Jewish Miscellanies

★★★★ UK

A wonderful collection of lists of Jewish names compiled by Jeffrey Maynard from diverse sources, such as synagogue records, and contributors to charities. Some of the larger lists, such as the London Jews database, transcribed from early trade directories, are hosted on the JewishGen.org site. Other lists include birth, marriage and death announcements culled from the Jewish Chronicle, extracts about life in the London Jewish communities in the mid-nineteenth century taken from Henry Mayhew's London Labour and the London Poor, which have been cross-referenced to the names and addresses of some of the families where known. Look out for the list of London Jewish publicans from the early twentieth century.

www.avotaynu.com
Avotaynu

★★★★ US

A publisher of works on Jewish genealogy, including books, microfiche, maps, CDs, and JPEGS of Jewish life in the Shtetls, as well as the International Review of Jewish Genealogy. Try the five-minute guide to Jewish Genealogy Research or subscribe to the free internet newsletter. The site is also home to the Consolidated Jewish Surname Index, with information about more than half-a-million surnames appearing in 34 different databases, all searchable.

www.orthohelp.com/geneal/sefardim.htm
Sephardic Genealogy Sources

★★★★ US

An excellent set of Sephardic links, organised by general sites, family pages, and then by country. Scroll further down the page for a list of articles about Sephardic genealogy and history, and ongoing projects, all compiled by Jeffrey S. Malka. Replace /sefardim.htm with /forms.htm in the URL, or use the menu from the original page to access Jewish Genealogy Forms and Sources, which includes a research planner, search log, bibliography, software notes and general genealogy links.

United States

As the majority of family history sites on the web originate in the US, this section is notably short. With American ancestors in your tree you are likely to gain much more benefit from the major commercial sites reviewed elsewhere, such as ancestry.com, and genealogy.com, as well as the sheer number of other researchers out there busily transcribing and sharing records online. You'll find everything from passenger lists from Mayflower onwards to special interest groups and mailing lists for almost every conceivable niche.

www.lr.org/code/home.htm
Lloyd's Register

★★★★★ US

For a straightforward, basic explanation of how more than 11-million people left Britain, many for the USA between 1815 and 1929, this can't be bettered. By far the quickest route to the relevant articles is to scroll to the bottom of the page and put the word 'immigration' into the search box.

www.genhomepage.com
The Genealogy Home Page

Overall rating: ★★★★★			
Classification:	Immigration	Readability:	★★★★★
Updating:	Regularly	Content:	★★★★
Navigation:	★★★★★	Speed:	★★★★★

US

This American site is most valuable for its function as an index of websites, particularly those devoted to North American records. It also lists a huge number of other websites worth consulting.

SPECIAL FEATURES

North American Genealogy Resources is a very helpful link that leads to a vast directory of relevant websites, starting with Canada, Mexico and the US in general, and moving on to more specialist information sources.

World-Wide Genealogy Resources is similarly well organised, listing genealogical resources alphabetically by country. Some of the sites listed, of course, are in the languages of the countries concerned.

Religious Genealogy Resources, Libraries and **Maps, Geography, Deeds and Photography** are other among the other useful links from the homepage.

With genealogical and family history research having now reached obsession levels in the US, a site of this kind, which collects all the relevant websites in one place and indexes them logically, is particularly welcome.

www.ellisislandrecords.org
Ellis Island On-Line

Overall rating: ★ ★ ★ ★ ★			
Classification: Immigration		**Readability:**	★ ★ ★ ★
Updating: Occasionally		**Content:**	★ ★ ★ ★
Navigation: ★ ★ ★		**Speed:**	★ ★ ★

US R £ ⓘ

A major addition to the online genealogy world since it launched its online searchable database in mid-April 2001, this site contains no fewer than twenty-two million entries, covering the period from 1892 to 1924, and has been made available thanks to support from the volunteers of the Church of Jesus Christ of the Latterday Saints, otherwise known as the Mormons.

Ellis Island was, of course, the processing centre for immigrants to the United States, and this has great interest for UK-based researchers who have American ancestors. It also, however, recorded all passengers entering the USA via the port of New York, even those who had only perhaps been away on holiday to such destinations as the Bahamas. Like many major sites, it suffered from overuse and was very slow or regularly inaccessible when it first launched. Happily it has settled down, and service levels are generally acceptable apart from at peak times, so it may be worth accessing this site in the mornings, before the US comes online.

From the homepage there are many links offering to part you from your money in various ways: spending in the family history gift shop, joining the Statue of Liberty–Ellis Island Foundation, inscribing your immigrant ancestor's name on the Wall of Honour. So far, so tacky. But don't let your sceptical hackles put you off at this point, as there are real records here. Keep your credit card in your pocket for a while

and head for the Passenger Search link section. Type in the first and last names of your immigrant ancestor, and gender. Search results can be organised by name, gender, year of arrival, ethnicity, age on arrival, port of departure, or name of ship. Use alternative spellings for your search (the site makes suggestions) as so many people altered their names after arrival, or were misunderstood at the point of entry.

When you have found a likely looking record, you can view the original ship's manifest with passenger names.

Widely recognised as a remarkable record of immigrants to America from the late-nineteenth century onwards, this is a valuable resoruce.

http://olivetreegenealogy.com/usa/index.shtml
The Olive Tree Genealogy

★ ★ ★ ★ ★ US

Links to just about all things American can be found here. The first and last half-dozen links from the homepage index are the ones that will reward investigation most, unless you know of a connection with a specific American state. If it doesn't appear that a successful transfer has been made, scroll down below the repeated index to find the relevant information.

Chapter 6

social groups

Once you have managed to establish what someone did for a living, it is worth investigating what resources are available on that particular trade or occupation. You may gain a clearer idea of how their days were spent, or find that there are specific work-related records on your particular ancestor. Many trades and professions have their own family history societies (see p. 40), and even more have relevant websites (try Google) and mailing lists where you can post queries and read tips for finding out more about that elusive ancestor. To find a relevant mailing list, go to http://lists.rootsweb.com

A promising development for those who are seaching ancestors who did not work, because they were sick, unable to support themselves, or in prison, is the Rossbret UK Webring (www.rossbret.pwp.blueyonder.co.uk), a very useful group of sites. These sites are proliferating and expanding the depth of their content, and several are mentioned in different parts of this chapter.

Those with more exalted lineages are well served on the web, with some very good sites dealing with royal and noble genealogies, and the associated art of heraldry.

Roman Catholics and nonconformist denominations often have thier own records outside the usual parish registers discussed in chapter 3. We therefore list some sites here to help point you in the right directions to find out about how and where these ancestors worshipped.

Occupational Terms

Censuses and BDM certificates tell us what our ancestors did to keep body and soul together, but often the terms used are rather obscure. If you need to know what an Accipitrary or a Ponderator did, try any of the following sites:

A List of Occupations
http://cpcug.org/user/jlacombe/terms.html

Ranks, Professions, Occupations and Trades
www.gendocs.demon.co.uk/trades.html

Old Occupation Names Index
www.rmhh.co.uk/occup.html

Colonial Occupation Titles and Definitions
www.rootsweb.com/~billingh/occupation.shtml

Obsolete Occupations
www.olivetreegenealogy.com/misc/occupations.shtml

Occupations

English Origins (see p. 31) has extensive apprenticeship records online covering 1568-1850.

www.pro.gov.uk/pathways/FamilyHistory
PRO Pathways to the Past

★★★★ UK

From the page on the PRO's site that this takes you to, select Gallery 2: People at Work to access introductions to the records available for Apprentices, Police, Customs and Excise, Coastguards, Lawyers in the Family, and Other Records about People at Work. The latter will help you find records of teachers, nurses, the military, bankrupts and people who have registered companies, businesses and patents. Other galleries cover the Army and Navy, Migrant Ancestors (including Britons abroad, evacuees, workhouses, pauper children and orphans sent abroad, refugees and immigrants), and Ancestors and the Law. Here you will find links and bibliographic information on specific trades and occupations.

www.genuki.org.uk/big/Occupations.html
England Occupations

★★★★ UK

Not as comprehensive as one might hope, but worth checking to see if the occupation you are interested in is covered. Seekers of Brickmakers and Innkeepers are in luck.

www.ruralhistory.org
Rural History Centre

★★★★ UK

Although this is a UK-based site, it is not reflected in the URL with the usual org.uk. The Rural History Centre at the University of Reading is the national centre in England for the study of the history of farming, food and the countryside. The value of the resource to the family historian is to help understand the lifestyle of the millions of agrarian workers whose lives go largely unrecorded. The Interface (INTERnet Farm And Countryside Explorer) resource is somewhat simplistic, even at the advanced level, so if you're trying to find out about life as a straw plaiter or farm labourer, head for the the online catalogue or the Bibliography of British and Irish Life, both found under Collections. Photographs is also worth a visit.

www.warwick.ac.uk/services/library/
University of Warwick Library

★★★★ UK

As a major repository for labour and industrial history records, the MRC has provided guides to the records available for carvers, compositors, gilders, house decorators, painters, picture-frame makers, printing workers, quarrymen, railwaymen and stonemasons. Go to the Catalogues section to find the link for the Modern Records Centre and then to Holdings and Catalogues, where the guides are listed. Links and On-line Resources is well worth a look too, especially if you are interested in the history of the labouring classes.

www.entertainer-genealogy.org.uk
The Circus, Theatre and Music Hall Families page

★★★★ US

Paul Newman (not that one) has provided an extraordinary resource for anyone researching ancestors who were actors, music hall and vaudeville artistes, travelling showmen, Romany/gypsies, circus performers, tinkers and travelling tradesmen. All of these groups can be very difficult to trace because of their peripatetic lifestyles. Particularly heroic are the extractions of records from various UK censuses, but there is plenty more to explore here as well.

Criminals

The lives of the working classes go largely unrecorded apart from when they were hatched, matched or despatched, or when they gave information of variable reliability to the census enumerators. The main exceptions occurred when they were unable to support themselves and ended up in workhouses or orphanages (see opposite), or when they came to the attention of the legal system. Many people who came up in front of a judge were of course innocent, or guilty of conduct that we would not nowadays consider a crime, but their supposed misdemeanours may be recorded nonetheless. Others were imprisoned or even deported to penal colonies. Given the dearth of other sorts of records, you may be very grateful for the odd black sheep in the family as these are often the only ones who leave a trace. The PRO (see p. 44) is the main repository for court and prison records, and their site contains several downloadable leaflets on these records, including Convicts and Prisoners 1100-1986. Some of the passenger list sites reviewed on p. 65 and in the Australian section also cover lists of convicts who were transported.

www.fred.net/jefalvey
Jeff Alvey Genealogy and Other Good Stuff

★★★★ US

Towards the bottom of the homepage there are links to Newgate Prison, with an introduction and list of inmates, victims and people associated with the prison. The Executions list covers the period from 1606-1895, but includes only the most notorious. See also www.law.utexas.edu/lpop/etext/completenewgate.htm to view the The Complete Newgate Calendar.

www.institutions.org.uk/prisons
Rossbret Prisons Website

★★★★ INT

From the homepage you can access prison history, a timeline, prison reports from 1837, 1839 and 1842. Most useful though are the sections for England, Scotland, Wales, and Ireland that link through to county-based listings of prison details. The nature and quantity of information submitted varies considerably, but this is nonetheless a promising resource.

www.southernx.com.au/convict.html
Convicts Transported to Australia

★★★★ AUS R 🔒

There are good links here to lists of convicts transported to Australia, but you need to pay to view the data held in the Southern Cross Library (AU$27.50 for six months). Highlights of the library include a complete listing of the Convict Transport Ships from England and Ireland to Australia, and Indexes for Convicts Transported to Australia between 1788 and 1868.

www.backtoroots.co.uk/page3.htm
Criminal Register Indexes (HO 27) by Stuart Tamblin

★★★★ UK

These indexes to persons charged with indictable offences in England and Wales between 1805 and 1892 are organised by county and are available on disk and fiche from Back To Roots (see p. 155 for details).

The Poor

Once again, the PRO's site is the place to turn for a leaflet on the Poor Law records available, or to search their online catalogue. For socio-historical background to the urban poor the Charles Booth site (p. 76) is an excellent source, and the Bolles Collection (p. 139) has the text of Henry Mayhew's London Labour and the London Poor online, as well as other works such as Degeneration amongst Londoners, and The Pauper, The Thief and The Convict. Local poor-law union and workhouse records are usually found in local record offices (see ARCHON p. 48)

www.workhouses.org.uk
The Workhouse

★★★★★ UK

A remarkably comprehensive site that covers its subject from every possible angle, with accessible prose and well-chosen pictures. An introduction to the Poor Laws is accompanied by the full text of the 1601 and 1834 Acts, the history of the Poor Law Unions, a tour of a workhouse and a detailed account of what life was like in them. Records and Archives gives a good overview of where to look for your ancestors' records. Education gives a run-down of all of the types of schools to which poor children had access before the state system was introduced. All the sections are worth visiting, even those not specifically mentioned here. It is hard to believe that this detailed and beautifully presented site is the work of one enthusiastic amateur, Peter Higginbotham, and it is a rewarding read for anyone, whether or not they have workhouse ancestors.

www.judandk.force9.co.uk/workhouse.html
The Union Workhouse

★★★★★ UK

The odd colours make this site slightly difficult to read, but there are good details and introductory material here, and an excellent set of links to other sites dealing with the poor, including individual workhouses.

www.genuki.org.uk/big/eng/Paupers
Index to 'Paupers in Workhouses 1861'

★★★★★ UK

A Parliamentary Paper of 1861 named around 14,000 adults who had lived in a workhouse for over five years and gave the reasons why they were unable to support themselves (usually age, infirmity or mental condition). On this site, George Bell has nobly indexed a 10% sample of the names in the Paper, together with the name of the workhouse and county, the reason for relief and term of relief. An excellent resource.

www.institutions.org.uk
Rossbret UK Institutions

★★★★★ UK

As well as plenty of background information on the Poor Laws, for example, this site gives a list of all the UK Poor Law Unions classified by county. Details include those parishes which contributed to a union, the population and area covered by the union, description of the workhouses, with numbers of insane, idiotic and imbecile inmates. Information about where the records for the union are now kept is provided. Similar detail is available for Asylums, Almshouses, Prisons, Dispensaries, Hospitals, Reformatories, Orphanages and Workhouses.

www.institutions.org.uk/counties/info/mailing_lists.htm
UK-WORKHOUSE-HOSP Mailing List Web Pages

★★★★★ UK

These pages support and provide links for the very active Workhouse and Hospitals mailing list. Here you willl find an excellent set of links on almshouses, asylums, hospitals, orphanages, prisons, schools, and workhouses.

http://dspace.dial.pipex.com/mbloy
A Web of English History

★★★★★ UK

Marcie Bloy's pages are of great interest in general but their period, that of George III (1760–1820, though the material here goes up to 1830) and of Sir Robert Peel (1830–1850) are so relevant to issues such as the Poor Law, Social Reform, Prisons and Public Health, that they belong in this section. This is a resource of great detail and exceptional value.

Hospitals and Asylums

Because of their inability to work, people with physical and mental problems were often found in workhouses and other institutions for the poor (see the previous section), and also swelled the ranks of people in prison (see p. 114). For those lucky enough to receive appropriate care, the following may provide routes to records or background information.

www.redcross.org.uk
British Red Cross

★★★★ UK

The four-star rating applies to the fact that this website is not of great practical use to genealogists, but the historical material available from the About Us link is useful as background material.

http://hospitalrecords.pro.gov.uk
Hospital Records Database

★★★★ UK

A joint project of the Wellcome Trust and the PRO, this database provides information on the existence and location of hospital records in the UK. There is a simple search facility that interrogates over 2800 hospital entries. From the data you can find the administrative details of the hospitals, and their status or type; the location and covering dates of administrative and clinical records; and the existence of lists, catalogues or other finding aids. Most records are closed for 100 years, unless there are strong reasons for access (genealogy doesn't count) and you have been referred by a doctor or social worker.

www.gendocs.demon.co.uk/institute.html
Victorian London Public Institutions

★★★★　UK

The list of Workhouses, Hospitals, Lunatic Asylums, Prisons, Barracks, Orphan Asylums, Convents and other Principal Charitable Institutions is a good place to get ideas for where to start looking for missing relatives in censuses.

www.melcombe.freeserve.co.uk/source/nurse list.htm
Angels & Orderlies

★★★　UK

These pages relate to the staff who served in Military Hospitals in the East during the Crimean War. There are good lists, though only further personal details about very few.

www.gmced.ac.uk/hn/history/index.htm
UK Centre for the History of Nursing

★★★　UK

A 'young' website seeking to preserve nursing records from all periods.

Child Migration

www.childmigrants.com
Child Migrants

★★★★　UK

A site dedicated to the emotive issue of the 130,000 British children removed from institutions and transported to Australia, Canada, New Zealand, South Africa and Zimbabwe between 1618 and 1970.

www.doh.gov.uk/childmigrants/index.htm
Former British Child Migrants

★★★　UK

The Department of Health's website hosts information on support for families seeking former child migrants. It gives contact details for the main Sending Agencies, such as Barnado's and The Catholic Child Welfare Council, who usually hold the birth records. Click through to the Information Index for details of the National Council of Voluntary Child Care Organisations' (NCVCCO) project to compile a Central Information Index, with basic information about each individual child for whom records still exist. The page also gives contact details for overseas organisations in the host countries.

Royals and Nobles

Many people have been motivated to trace their genealogy by old family rumours of great-great-great-great grandparents who were the illegitimate offspring of a naughty young prince or duke. Though these stories are rarely substantiated, we can take comfort in the latest genetic theories, based on the research by Dr Brian Sykes. This suggests that all the peoples of Europe are descended from seven women, so we are all much more closely related genetically than was previously suspected. And in any case, every family tree, if it can be traced back widely enough and far enough, will link with a royal line eventually.

www.worldroots.com
The Royalty Pages

★★★★   US

Created by Brigitte Gastel Lloyd out of a fascination for her own royal and other notable connections, this is a huge database of information about the Royal dynasties of Europe and even some further afield. Use the Site Map and General Index page for an overview. At the bottom of the homepage is a very sophisticated search facility which came up trumps when tested with an obscure eighteenth-century noble. From here you can also access numerous databases including the European Royalty and Nobility from A to Z. A very worthwhile specialist site for any research into royal connections.

www.baronage.co.uk
The Baronage Press

★★★★   UK

The Baronage Press offers information to help people establish connections with noble lines, or more often disabuse them of the notion that they might have such connections. The online magazine, The Baronage, is available to read, covering a wide range of genealogical and heraldic topics, with some very good illustrations. Or you can sign up for an email newsletter, The Feudal Herald. Do scroll down to the Editor's Notes on the bottom of the homepage, which exposes the many 'scams' that are prevalent on the internet and direct mail, peddling false coats of arms and noble titles.

www.genuki.org.uk/big/eng/History/Barons/
The English Peerage 1790

★★★★   UK

The arrival page lists the family names of various Viscounts and Barons, and refers to you to the relevant file for a group of names. Within the files there are full transcriptions from the 1790 edition of The English Peerage, a view of the Ancient and Present State of the English Nobility.

www.dcs.hull.ac.uk/public/genealogy
Royal and Noble Genealogical Data on the Web

★★★★   UK

Brian Tompsett in the department of Computer Science at Hull University maintains this website, which lists all the sources of genealogical data about royal families (British and other). A quick run through the extensive index on the homepage will give an immediate idea of the vast amount of material available. Links load relatively slowly, but some are well worth waiting for. They are usefully divided into those sites that are, and are not, of genealogical relevance. As there are over 30,000 individuals in the database of people linked to the British royal family via blood or marriage, this is a good place to try to substantiate those family myths. The site also includes details of all English peerages, searchable by name, date or title.

www.royal.gov.uk
The British Monarchy

★★★   UK

The official website of the British monarchy is attractive and well presented but likely to be of little use to genealogical researchers except for tracing their descent once they have 'collided' with a royal line (which all family trees, if traced laterally and sufficiently far back in time, inevitably do). For these purposes click on History of the Monarchy.

www.burkes-peerage-baronetage.com
Burke's Peerage and Gentry

★★★   UK

Heavily commercialised since its move to US ownership, Burke still has value because the actual Burke's volumes remain a central resource. You can view a basic, current record online for free, but you have to pay to see a full lineage.

Heraldry

The most important sites on this subject offer relatively little by way of online information, and so the College of Arms and the Institute of Heraldic and Genealogical Studies are both reviewed on p. 170. The key point to remember is that coats of arms are personal to individuals, and not to everyone with a particular surname. Beware then of any advertisement, even on recommended sites, that offers you any paraphenalia emblazoned with 'your' coat of arms.

www.heraldica.org
Heraldica

★★★★   US

Heraldica covers its subject thoroughly: national heraldry is discussed by country, from Austria to Zambia, with special sections devoted to the US, Britain and France, academic and ecclesiastical heraldry, the language and origins, with an illustrated glossary of over 500 terms. The section on Royalty, Nobility, and Knighthood and Chivalry looks at origins, succession laws, styles, precedence, titles, nobiliary law and customs. Round this off with a good set of international links and this is as good a place as any to start. The best way in is via the Site Map, found from Topics discussed at this Site.

www.digiserve.com/heraldry
Heraldry on the Internet

★★★   US

There are many links on this site offering dubious merchandise, but one or two features, such as Pimbley's Dictionary of Heraldry, and the links classfied in the long menu down left-hand side of the page, are worth a look.

The Established Church

Church of England parish records have been dealt with at length on pp. 58-59.

www.genuki.org.uk/big/ChurchRecords.html
United Kingdom and Irelands Church Records

★★★★★ UK

As usual GENUKI is the best starting point, both for background information and relevant links.

www.lambethpalacelibrary.org
Lambeth Palace Library

★★★★★ UK

This is the only remotely five-star website (apart from GENUKI) that could be listed here. Click first on Library Holdings and then on Introduction to Holdings before moving to Guides to Sources for Research. There is plenty to explore even though, as the site explains, there may not be much directly genealogical material.

www.cofe.anglican.org
The Church of England Website

★★★★ UK

There is little of direct interest to the genealogist here, though sections within About the Church of England, covering organisation, history and built heritage, provide useful background information.

www.churchinwales.org.uk
The Church in Wales

★★★★ UK

Select the language of your choice to enter. The Clergy and Parish Database is useful for establishing which parish churches might be relevant for your searches, and there is a clear map of the Dioceses. There are links to each of the parishes that has its own website in Parishes Online, and the main Links section has a short list specifically on Genealogies.

www.ireland.anglican.org
The Church of Ireland

★★★★ UK

Like most official sites in Ireland, this site is very aware of the needs of family historians and there is a link for Genealogy right on the home page, marked in red, leading to details of how to consult parish registers, and information about the Representative Church Body Library, the main source for Irish parish registers, archives and manuscripts.

www.scotland.anglican.org
The Scottish Episcopal Church

★★★ UK

Each of the seven Scottish Dioceses has its own homepage with details of and links to its churches.

www.churchofscotland.org.uk
The Church of Scotland Online

★★★ UK

Click on Site Map (top of page) and then explore the Serving Scotland link to access an explanation of the organisation of the Church of Scotland and the list of online parishes.

Roman Catholics

www.catholic-history.org.uk
Catholic History
★★★ UK

This umbrella site houses pages for a number of distinct societies and individuals with an interest in Catholic history in the British Isles since the Reformation. There are links from the main Catholic History homepage to regional Catholic History societies, and the following:

Catholic Family History Society
www.catholic-history.org.uk/cfhs
Sparse information about membership of the society and its activities, though Services gives a good idea of the indexes and resources compiled by the Society.

The Catholic Record Society
www.catholic-history.org.uk/crs
The introduction warns explicity that the Society does not have genealogical interests and cannot help those researching their family trees, but it has nonetheless published a wide range of materials illustrating the history and culture of the British Catholics, many of which name names, so it is worth taking a look. The detailed contents and indexes give a good idea of what may be relevant.

The Catholic Archives Society
www.catholic-history.org.uk/catharch
The main interest here is the Directory of Catholic Archives, which gives addresses of archives of dioceses and religious orders,and details of how to obtain it.

Latin Place-names
www.catholic-history.org.uk/latin_names.htm
A useful list giving modern equivalents of Latin place names.

www.catholic-library.org.uk
The Catholic Central Library
★★★ UK

Based near Euston Station in London, the library houses a large collection of Catholic-themed literature including a family history collection. Most important is the collection of Mission Registers (the equivalent of parish records), and details of dates and parishes covered are available online. The reading rooms are open to the public, but you need to be a member to borrow books.

http://home.att.net/~Local_Catholic
Local Catholic Church and Family History Research Guide
★★★ US

Typography and layout make this site difficult to use, but the material is good: guides to the types of records that may be found and to the locations of records are necessarily general given that this site caters for Catholics worldwide, but there are specific sections for each country which leads on to very detailed information and links about individual dioceses and parishes.

www.catholic-church.org.uk
Catholic-church.org
★★★ US

This is not an official site but provides quick links to the national websites for England and Wales and Scotland, plus Alapadre's links to diocesan and parish websites, and the English language version of the Vatican website.

Nonconformists

By 1851, 25% of the population were nonconformists but the records are sparse, and relatively little information is available on the internet apart from a few registers that were filmed for the IGI. Until 1837 the only legally recognised marriages performed outside the Church of England were those of Quakers and Jews, so the vast majority of people, whatever their religious beliefs, will appear in the C of E parish registers before that date. A large collection of nonconformist registers (including some Presbyterian, Congregational and Baptist records) and indexes is housed at Dr Williams's Library in London, but the library is not yet online. Others are held by the PRO and the FRC (see the PRO catalogue and the FRC leaflet on How to Use: Nonconformist Registers). For Huguenots see p. 101 and for Jews see pp 106-7.

www.qfhs.co.uk
Quaker Family History Society

★★★★★ UK

This site provides more detail on its site than most family history societies, with very good introductions to the types of records available online in the Research section, and links to Quaker sources. Contents includes county-by-county listings of where the Meeting Records are located.

www.geocities.com/Heartland/pointe/4320/m_1.html
Methodist Ministers and Probationers

★★★★ UK

Christine Amsden has compiled an index of men who trained for the Methodist ministry in the UK between 1870 and 1936, and links to other Methodist source information. She also has a list dating back to the 1700s which she will consult on request.

www.gendocs.demon.co.uk/bapt.html
Victorian London Churches Baptist Union

★★★★ UK

As well as a long list of Baptist churches extracted from Dickens's Dictionary of London 1888, this article gives a good introduction to the various factions, and where the records are held.

Chapter 7

war and the services

The first port of call for anyone researching an ancestor who served in the British Army, Navy, Royal Marines or Merchant Navy must be the Public Record Office at Kew (see p.44).

Army Lists have been published almost annually since 1754, though, unfortunately, many records were lost in a bombing raid during the Second World War. The earliest Navy Records date back to the mid-seventeeth century. Both groups of records are held at the PRO.

Records from the two World Wars are held at the Family Records Centre (see p. 43) and current, or very recent, service records are held at the Ministry of Defence (see www.mod.uk). Recent and current records, however, are not normally available to the general public.

In addition to these national holdings, there are several other good collections. The websites that follow are all of a noticeably high standard and will thoroughly reward exploration. It is important when searching for a particular ancestor, rather than merely seeking information about the wider historical picture, that you are as accurate as possible about the name, dates of service and regiment or ship(s) with which your ancestor was associated.

www.cwgc.org
Commonwealth War Graves Commission

★★★★★ UK

Invariably listed as one of the best sites on the Web, this is a model of clarity and elegance. The various items in the Contents column down the left of the page include The Task, Horticulture, Architecture, Global Commitment and a profile of Sir Fabian Ware, who was responsible for the idea of the Commission. On the right of the page, meanwhile, is the search facility for the Debt of Honour Register, which is probably where you want to be.

SPECIAL FEATURES

Debt of Honour Register will search almost regardless of how limited the information you give, particularly if the surname you are searching for is not too common. Note, though, that using an initial in the second box may cause problems unless you are absolutely certain of it, because the computer selects only those names for whom the given initial comes first. If the person you are seeking was commonly known by a second name and you enter that initial, you will not find the right connection.

Each time a record is found, it gives details of rank, number, force, date of death and age. It also gives details of parents (if known) and approximate address (town and county), spouse if married, and may give a little more by way of education or profession. Finally, it gives details of the cemetery where the casualty is buried and basic directions for finding it. At the bottom of this page the Display Record of Commemoration link takes you to the actual inscription.

At this point, it may be worth going back to Services and Links in the Contents column to see what further information may be available from the Commission, now that you have better details of the casualty you are seeking.

For instance, the exact location of individual graves is normally available, and you may wish to click on the link to The Royal British Legion, for example, which helps arrange visits to war graves. Other links on the same page include The Imperial War Museum, The German War Graves Commission, Australian War Memorial and many others.

For anyone seeking details of a wartime casualty from any date from the First World War onwards, this is an invaluable resource, clearly and helpfully presented.

www.veteransagency.mod.uk
Ministry of Defence – Veterans' Agency

★★★ UK

While the MOD will not be of much use in general to genealogists, this internal website dealing with all matters concerning veterans may be helpful.

www.kcl.ac.uk/lhcma/top.htm
King's College London Liddell Hart Centre for Military Archives

★★★★★ UK

Based around the library collections of Captain Sir Basil Liddell Hart, the Centre now holds the archives of around 600 distinguished 20th-century British defence personnel.

SPECIAL FEATURES

For internal research purposes, you are invited to give your name and the reason for visiting the site, but this is entirely voluntary.

What Can You Find Here? briefly introduces the collections.

List of the Collections is more informative, starting with a long list of the papers pertaining to each individual, listed alphabetically by name. The contents of some, but not all, of these can be consulted in more detail by clicking on the words 'detailed catalogue' in blue alongside the relevant entries. Following this is a list of other documents, catalogued by title, of which basic details are available online.

What do I have to do to Consult Original Material? explains the necessarily slightly restricted access that is available, and which requires a letter of recommendation from a suitable referee. No actual records can be consulted online, so a visit in person is necessary.

Excellent, sometimes remarkable, material is available here for the family historian seeking to build up a picture of war during the 20th century.

http://link.bubl.ac.uk/link/search.html
BUBLink Search

★★★★★ UK

Strathclyde University's BUBL Information Service becomes more impressive daily. Click on BUBL Search and then on Search BUBL Link for the search facility. Keep your query as simple as possible, so for the purposes of this section merely enter 'war' in the simple search and select Subject Terms, and you will move to an excellent directory of links.

www.lib.byu.edu/~rdh/wwi/
The World War 1 Document Archive

★★★★★ UK

Assembled by volunteers of the World War 1 Military History List, this site presents primary documents concerning the Great War in all its aspects. An excellent source for

background research, and the family historian can use the search box for a name search of every document on the site.

Already a remarkable resource, and this is just the beginning.

www.remembrancetravel.com
Remembrance Travel

★★★★★ UK

The title is self-explanatory and this area of the British Legion's service is growing rapidly, and may be of real interest to family historians. The Legion's annual Poppy Day is well known and its own website is at www.britishlegion.org.uk, though it cares for those suffering the effects of war today rather than containing any historical material.

www.mick-gray.co.uk/military_sites.htm
Military Sites

★★★★ UK

This is merely a list of websites but an interesting list starting with the Accrington Pals and ending with a list of teh eight names inscribed on the Wyberton Memorial WWII. Mick Gray, as the home button at the bottom of the page tells you, is also a genealogist, so his interest is from that angle.

www.iwm.org.uk
Imperial War Museum

Overall rating: ★ ★ ★ ★			
Classification: Museum		**Readability:**	★ ★ ★ ★
Updating: Occasionally		**Content:**	★ ★ ★
Navigation: ★ ★		**Speed:**	★ ★ ★

This site links to the museums that come under the IWM's administration, including the Cabinet War Rooms and HMS Belfast as well as the main museum in London. The principal areas of interest for the family historian, however, are found in the Collections section.

SPECIAL FEATURES

Family History Research provides a short guide to researching the collections. There are leaflets available in PDF form on tracing ancestors from different branches of the services, plus details of events to introduce the collections to researchers. Special sections on Rolls of Honour, of which the museum has a collection of over 80 volumes, and Gallantry Awards and Commissions, suggest further areas of research. The Links section is definitely worth a visit.

UK National Inventory of War Memorials is a huge project to compile a database of the estimated 54,000 war memorials throughout the UK commemorating all conflicts. Unfortunately the material has not been put online, and the first phase of project has not collected names, but here you will find details about how to access the collection in person.

Stronger on background information than actual records, but good resources nonetheless.

www.genuki.org.uk/big/MilitaryRecords.html
United Kingdom and Ireland Military Records

The surprise here is how few sites are listed as there appear to be very few transcriptions of military indexes available on the web. Nonetheless it is worth taking a look, just in case one of your ancestors was a Dock Yard Volunteer or was listed in the Naval and Military Almanac for 1840. By far the most useful part of the page though is the complete listing with links to the many PRO leaflets about the various service records they hold, dating back to 1522.

www.users.dircon.co.uk/~searcher
Public Record Searches by Bob O'Hara

Bob O'Hara specialises in searching the records at the PRO to find military ancestors. As well as listing his areas of expertise, he gives a good introduction to the nature of the records held and what information you might find, which will provide research ideas if you decide to go it alone.

www.fhindexes.co.uk
Family History Indexes

★ ★ ★ ★   UK

The indexes are available on microfiche, floppy disks or CD-rom. They include Military Courts, Militia Musters and Royal Naval History. Stuart Tamblin, a family historian specialising in military and nineteenth-century criminal research, has his homepage listed in links.

http://forcesreunited.org.uk
Forces Reunited

★★★★ UK

This is effectively a people-finder for former comrades in arms. There is no historical material here.

Army

www.regiments.org
Land Forces of Britain, the Empire and Commonwealth

★★★★ UK

This website explains in detail the British regimental system throughout the world, past and present. It is a vital resource for anyone researching an ancestor who served in the army. For genealogists it has two uses: first, it gives information about the structure and practice of the army within a military history context, and, second, it helps you track down recent ancestors who may have served in the army. The homepage explains that there are several thousand links from this website 'bringing together all internet resources pertaining to land forces that were at any time part of the British Empire or Commonwealth'. Naval and air forces are not included in the site, except where they have land-force elements. Use the Site Map tab at the top of the page to get started.

www.lightinfantry.org.uk
British Light Infantry Regiments

★★★★★ CAN

At the top of the homepage is a long list of links for each of the light-infantry regiments covered. Within each regiment's section a fresh set of links appears, offering well-ordered background information. Search only introduces you to Google but Links is worth trying.

http://members.ozemail.com.au/~clday
Family History in India

★★★★ AUS

Scroll down the homepage to the Regimental Histories button for a number of British Army units that served in India. Cathy Day also provides the lineages of all the British Army Infantry Regiments, detailing all the amalgamations and name changes through the years. This is of interest to anyone searching for infantrymen, whether or not they served in India. The further links are also very useful.

www.army.mod.uk
The British Army

★★★★ UK

From the homepage head via Ceremonial and Heritage to Units and Organisations which gives information on and connections to the sites for individual regiments. Some of these have good historical information, though the amount of detail varies considerably. As this is part of the Ministry of Defence site, it is primarily concerned with contemporary issues.

www.tdrake.demon.co.uk/infantry.htm
British Infantry Name Changes 1881

★★★★ UK

This site explains that a major reform of the British Army took place in 1881, giving each infantry regiment a county affiliation. A table gives the pre-1881 regimental number and the regiment's name after the reforms.

Royal Navy and other sailors

www.port.nmm.ac.uk
PORT: Maritime Information Gateway

★★★★　UK

The National Maritime Museum has produced a massive portal of maritime resources. You can browse by subject category or historical period, or search the database. As yet though there are no dedicated resources for the family historian, though many of the catalogue entries for material held elsewhere (such as the PRO) are very helpful. The amount of material within any given section is often so great that sub-indexing into categories, rather than straight alphabetical listing, is now needed. It also makes page loading noticeably slow.

www.royal-navy.mod.uk
The Royal Navy Website

★★★★　UK

The Royal Navy part of the MOD's website also provides access to material for the Fleet Air Arm, Submarines and the Royal Marines. RN Profile leads to sections on organisation, history, uniforms and badges, flags and pennants. Links is tucked away at the top of the page, and are mostly to other MOD or government sites, but there are a few worth exploring.

www.genuki.org.uk/big/MerchantMarine.html
United Kingdom and Ireland Merchant marine

★★★★　UK

Those looking for mariners fare rather better on Genuki than on the Military Records page listed above, with plenty of links to online records.

www.angelfire.com/de/BobSanders/Site.html
Tracing British Seamen And Their Ships

★★★★　UK

Bob Sanders has collected together research guides to tracing every conceiveable type of seafarer, from harbour pilots to fishermen, coastguards, Customs and Excise officers as well as members of the Royal Navy and merchant seamen. The Maritime links initially seem sparse, but click on the red lettering for Some More Useful Maritime Links, and the list that appears is exhaustive.

www.mariners-L.co.uk
Mariners List Website

★★★★　UK

This is the website to accompany the active Mariners mailing list, for people 'researching the mariners and ships of the merchant marine and the world's navies'. You can join the list from here, or view the links and research guides assembled by country. The UK research guides written by Debbie Beavis are largely the ones reproduced on Bob Sander's site (above), though less clearly presented here, and the links refer you back to Bob's site. Other sections are more worthwhile though, such as the list of links to Ship Companies, the information on the East India Company, and the booklist. Do visit Debbie Beavis' own site (www.beavis.co.uk) where she is assembling databases of names, including passenger lists.

RAF

www.raf.mod.uk
The Royal Airforce Internet Site

★★★★   UK

The main areas of interest here for the family historian are History, and Units and Stations, both accessible from the Menu Options, and the Veterans and Ex-Serviceman's Contacts (a text link in the centre of the page). The Battle of Britain and RAF Picture Library and many other images are found from On Display in the Menu Options, and then Picture Gallery. Aircraft are identified by placing your cursor over the images without clicking.

Medals

www.britishmilitarymedals.co.uk
A Collector's Guide to British Military Medals

★★★★   UK

Although there are still some gaps here, this is a great resource for viewing, identifying and understanding medals. It gives detailed information and the photographs, where available, are excellent.

www.arbeia.demon.co.uk
Militaria on the Web

★★★   UK

You will probably find this site easier to use if you first of all go into View at the top of the page, scroll down to Text Size and select Largest. You can now read the left-of-page index more easily. Collectors' Guides opens a page that includes British Gallantry & Campaign Medals, and each 'further details' button produces an explanation of what that medal was awarded for, usually with a photograph.

www.medal.net
MedalNet

★★★★   NZ

A portal for researchers and collectors of Orders, Decorations and Medals awarded by British Commonwealth countries, with a good set of links to medal-related websites.

www.collectionofcollections.com
Collection of Collections

★★★   UK

The militaria links available here range worldwide and, despite some broken links and no apparently very recent updating, form an exceptional resource. Choose the See Them link and select from there. Police Insignia and Toy Soldiers are available too.

Uniforms

www.capefam.freeserve.co.uk
Military Images

★★★★★ UK

Roger Capewell's site contains over 4000 photographs of unidentified servicemen, with descriptions to help identify the subject or their uniforms. There are several other archives of images including a war memorial collection, and Indian Army uniforms, and articles, information (including lists of names) and free look-up services.

www.militarybadges.org.uk
Military Badges

★★★★★ UK

This Roger Capewell site, a partner to Military Images above, offers suggestions for searching for, and identifying badges. You can browse the images, organised by Infantry, Cavalry, Corps and Navy, or if you know the regiment, there are alphabetical lists. It is also possible to order replica badges from the site.

www.militaryheritage.com/magazine.htm
Military Heritage

★★★★★ CAN

Military Heritage mainly sells replica weapons and uniforms but it also publishes a well-designed internet magazine with articles on pre-20th century, mostly British, military uniforms, swords and instruments. Good Links lead from each section to war museums and military enthusiasts' sites.

Chapter 8

online resources

Of course, every site reviewed in this book is an online resource, but this section is a pot pourri of the wonderfully diverse sites that can be invaluable to the family historian. Unlike the majority of genealogy sites, they are not concerned with records, but rather with putting some flesh on the bones of the names and dates. They will help you solve a problem, decipher historical handwriting, translate Latin records, date a photograph, find a location, work out what someone's legacy was worth in today's money or interpret what they died of. It's like having a whole reference library at your fingertips.

As many of these sites are run by individuals and are therefore prone to come and go, we have started the section with a review of Google, the best site for tracking down where sites have moved to or finding further sources of arcane information. It is the ultimate online resource and the family historian's best friend.

www.google.co.uk
Google

Overall rating: ★ ★ ★ ★ ★			
Classification: Search		**Readability:**	★ ★ ★ ★ ★
Updating: Continuously		**Reliability:**	★ ★ ★ ★ ★
Navigation: ★ ★ ★ ★ ★		**Speed:**	★ ★ ★ ★ ★

US

This site has become the most successful internet search engine by word of mouth, because it does what it sets out to do beautifully, simply and fast. It has become the genealogists' friend to such an extent people often refer on message boards to time spent 'googling', just searching the net for the pure pleasure of the unexpected gems it turns up.

Just type the words you want to search into the single box on the clean page. You can choose to search the whole of the web or UK sites only. It is also possible to search images, groups and a directory (which draws on Yahoo's editor-compiled listings). Google's search assumes that you want all the words to appear in a document, unless you specify otherwise. If you want a particular phrase to appear, enclose it in quotation marks.

Idle searching for names will often bring surprisingly useful results, though it can be difficult if you are looking for very common names such as William Smith, or names that are commonly occurring words, such as Wood or White. In these cases try combinining the search with words such as genealogy, family history, or something else you know about the person, like their occupation or where they were born, to narrow down the search. Don't forget to try variant spellings.

Google is wonderful for tracing information of any sort, and the use you can put it to is limited only by your imagination.

http://homepages.rootsweb.com/~hornbeck
Shirley Hornbeck's This and That Genealogy Tips

★★★★　US

Although the site does not appear to have been updated for some time, it is a mine of genealogical tidbits and good sense, partly culled from a book by Shirley Hornbeck. The pages cover topics such as African-American genealogy, black Dutch and Irish, Melungeons, Moravians and Pennsylvanian Dutch, Canada, cemeteries, censuses, Civil War (American), copyright, death records, definitions and abbreviations, diseases, medical terms, epidemics, email and the internet, England, Scotland and Ireland, Europe, GEDCOM, Gemany, Getting Started, HTML pedigree chart and family group sheet, immigration and passports, LDS and FHCs, microfilm, miscellaneous, myths, naming patterns, national archives, occupations, photographs, probate records and wills, Prussia and Poland, relationship chart, religion, wars and military information, and various other mainly US-related subjects. So there's probably something for everyone here!

www.any-web.co.uk
ANY-web

★★★　US

This UK-focused search engine claims that it is already receiving 16 million hits a year. Its genealogy section is as yet fairly limited but the sites it does list are a sound selection. Keep an eye on this one.

Buildings and Cemeteries

As well as the sites listed below, take a look at the COLLAGE site on p.77, which has a large selection of prints from the Guildhall Collection online. Wartime cemeteries are in the Military pages, starting on p.123.

www.imagesofengland.org.uk
Images of England

★★★★   UK   R

A project run by the National Monuments Record with English Heritage, this database is working to create photographs and detailed descriptions of over 370,000 listed buildings and monuments, and is being added to regularly. You can use the Quicksearch immediately, which limits you to 50 search results, or register to use the Advanced search. The search mechanism is somewhat clumsy for narrowing down what you need, but the results are worth the effort.

www.rcahms.gov.uk
Royal Commission on the Ancient and Historical Monuments of Scotland

★★★★   UK   R

Once again Scotland was very quick to put its records online with CANMORE, the searchable database of the National Monuments Record of Scotland, providing information on architectural, archaeological and maritime sites throughout Scotland. You need to register to use the search facility.

www.images-of-London.co.uk
Images of London

★★★★   UK

A database of sepia photographs, prints and watercolours of London. Copies can be ordered online.

www.francisfrith.com
The Francis Frith Collection

★★★★   UK

This commercial site sells prints from a collection of photographs of over 7000 towns and villages in Britain, dating from 1860 onwards. Preview images of the photographs can be viewed on the site and are indexed by county or can be searched by subject.

www.gravestonephotos.com
Gravestone Photograph Resource

★★★   UK

As yet very limited in scope, which explains that star-rating, this could become extremely useful. They need many more volunteers.

http://ancestorsreunited.com
Ancestors Reunited

★★★   UK

Throughout the UK, photographers and researchers will seek out and record for you the details of family gravestones. You can email for a quotation.

Other Cemetery-recording websites include:

www.cemeteryfriends.fsnet.co.uk
www.mausolea-monuments.org.uk
www.saving-graves.co.uk
www.gerrypalliser.co.uk
http://interment.net

Calendars

http://privatewww.essex.ac.uk/~kent/calisto
Calisto

★★★★ UK

Here you will find a downloadable program that converts dates from the Gregorian to the Julian calendar. It is accompanied by a list of the dates on which different countries and states made the change. The glossary will help you tell the difference between Rogation Days and Bissextile years. Feast days are listed alphabetically and numerically.

www.genfair.com/dates.htm
Old Style and New Style Dates

★★★★ UK

A useful guide to the potential pitfalls for family historians in interpreting dates in old documents.

www.albion.edu/english/calendar/regnal.htm
Regnal Year Calculator

★★★★ UK

This little program converts dates expressed as a year in a monarch's reign into ordinary AD dates. The calculator works from William I to George I.

Currency converters

www.ex.ac.uk/~RDavies/arian/current/howmuch.html
Current Value of Old Money

★★★★ UK

A very useful site if you have a will or trading documents that refer to sums of money, and want to work out what the equivalent value would be today. Some of the calculators refer to foreign measures, but the How Much is that Worth Today? link offers the Purchasing Power of the British Pound 1600 to Present. Inflation rates for the US and Great Britain, and Exchange rate between the United States dollar and the British pound 1791-2000 are particularly worth a mention. For example a legacy of £46 in 1700 would have the purchasing power of £4210 today.

www.rmhh.co.uk
The Hall Genealogy Website

★★★★ US

The public-spirited Halls have collected a number of useful resources and links together on this site (including lists of old occupations, medical terms, Latin terms, passenger lists, military links and a very well-compiled set of resources on mariners), from which you should select Shopper's Currency Converter, powered by XE.com. The currency converter is useful for those who are sending for genealogy material from overseas, as the conversion rates are live, and so always accurate.

Events

http://users.ox.ac.uk/~malcolm/genuki/geneva
GENEVA – The GENUKI calendar of GENealogical EVents and Activites

★★★★　US

Jointly run on behalf of GENUKI and the Federation of Family History Societies, this is probably the most comprehensive listing of events of interest to genealogists and family historians, with links to sites where you can gain more information about a particular event. All SoG events are listed, and there are links to a number of societies that regularly organise events both in the UK and internationally.

http://members.aol.com/aquarterma/familyhistoryfairs.html
Family History Fairs

★★★★　US

These fairs move around the country and have up to one hundred stall-holders, often including the Society of Genealogists, The Guild of One Name Studies, Back to Roots, local family history societies, and many specialist vendors. At the site you can find the dates and participants in forthcoming events.

Finding people online

The people in question here are the living: these are facilities to help you trace missing persons, such as relations you have lost touch with, or distant cousins you never had contact with but have discovered in the course of your genealogical researches. The simplest way to try to track someone down is to enter their name in a search engine such as google.com. Narrow the search by trying the name in combination with any words that you associate with the person, such as the place where they live or work, or a hobby they participate in.

www.friendsreunited.co.uk
Friends Reunited

★★★★　UK　R　🔒

The phenomenal success of this simple idea makes it all the more useful. People register for all the schools they attended. By paying £5 registration for full membership you can send messages to other members and add items to the message boards.

www.192.com
192.com

★★★★　UK　R　🔒

192 bills itself as the largest UK directory enquiry service, but it offers rather more than that. As well as phone numbers, they have a people finder, business finder and the most up-to-date electoral rolls. You can also access international directories. Up to ten simple searches are free, but more complex ones require a subscription.

GEDCOM files

GEnealogical Data COMmunication (which is what GEDCOM stands for) is a standard file format that allows different genealogy programs to exchange data. If you want to share your files, or import data from somebody else's family tree, it is very helpful to understand what they are and how they work.

www.cyndislist.com/gedcom.htm
Cyndi's GEDCOM List

★★★★★ US

Starting with a good explanation of the uses for GEDCOM files, this goes on to list general resource sites (for creating charts, converting dates, splitting and analysing files, tutorials etc); GEDCOM to HTML conversion, and viewers, which will allow you to read or browse GEDCOMS if you don't have a family history software program to import the files into.

www.my-ged.com
David Wilks' Free GEDCOM Server

★★★★ US

This website has an excellent set of FAQs, the first of which contains a link to Jan McClintock's GEDCOM101, which takes you step-by-step through the basics of understanding and using GEDCOM files.

Handwriting

www.amberskyline.com/treasuremaps/oldhand
Deciphering Old Handwriting

★★★★ US

Extracted from a course taught by Sabina J. Murray, this very useful introduction gives examples of changes in letters and discussion of issues such as phonetic spelling, old style abbreviations, personal marks and archaic numbers. There is also a handwriting puzzle to unravel, providing a salutary lesson in how even experts can be tripped up.

http://ourworld.compuserve.com/homepages/dave_tylcoat/handwrit.htm
Early English Handwriting

★★★★ UK R 🔒

Maintained by Dave and Sue Tylcoat, this website illustrates the problem of reading early handwriting, using a number of examples taken from the sixteenth and seventeenth centuries. Below the examples is succinct advice on how to get started with an old document. There is also a link to a glossary of unfamiliar words that crop up in old documents.

Further help may be found from:

www.scottishdocuments.com
Scottish Documents
http://freespace.virgin.net/dave.postles/palindex.html
An Introduction to Palaeography
www.jaydax.co.uk/genlinks/palaeography.html
Palaeography – Reading Early Writing
http://freebmd.rootsweb.com/handwriting.html
Reading the Writing

Latin

www.quicklatin.com
Quick Latin

★★★★ US

Here you can download a tool that helps you translate Latin into English, for Windows-compatible computers only. It is a shareware program that you can try for 30 days free of charge and thereafter pay $29 (£20). Secure online payment facilities are available.

http://sunsite.ubc.ca/LatinDictionary/index.html
The Online Latin-English/English-Latin Dictionary

★★★★ US

You can choose from a searchable Java applet or HTML version (in effect, an alphabetised word list) of the dictionary. Simple, straightforward and very usable.

www.familysearch.org/Eng/Search/RG/guide/WLLatin.asp
Family Search Latin Genealogical Word List

★★★★ US

Go to Search, Research Guidance, England, and then Latin Genealogical Word List. This provides a good introduction to the basics of Latin, as well as words you are likely to come across in genealogical sources. It also gives translations for numbers, dates and time.

Legal terms

http://users.rcn.com/deeds/legal.htm
Legal Terms in Land Records

★★★★★ UK

Specifically aimed at genealogical users struggling to cope with the archaic and unfamiliar terms used in land records, this extremely comprehensive list explains such obscurities as Fieri Facias and Feoffees.

www.uklegal.com/articles/latin.htm
Clickdocs Legal Glossary

★★★★ UK

English and Latin terms in common use in law.

www.pls2000.co.uk/glossary.htm
Glossary of Legal Terms and Latin Maxims

★★★ UK

An inelegant but functional resource.

Maps: modern

http://uk.multimap.com
Multimap

★★★★★ UK

Subtitled 'a complete Interactive Atlas on the Web', this will easily help you to find where your ancestors lived, and which places nearby they might have moved to, or to find your way to a records office in an unfamiliar part of the world. Use the Quicksearch box to put in the name or the postcode to produce a map. To enlarge the scale, either alter the scale figure in the drop-down box, moving to a lower number, or simply click successively on the relevant area; for wider view move to a higher number. Use the arrow to explore adjacent maps. At any time you can click on Local Info to view associated websites, though these can be disappointing. Directions allows you to put in a starting point and destination, and it will produce road directions within Great Britain. Aerial Photos are provided in association with Getmapping, and are available for most of England and parts of Wales in a 1:10,000 scale.

www.streetmap.co.uk
Streetmap

★★★★★ UK

Streetmap provides address searching and street map facilities for the whole of mainland Britain, and similar functionality to Multimap, though the maps appear more detailed than those on Multimap, going down to a scale of 1:2,500. This would be the top choice for detailed maps, particularly of London.

www.ordsvy.gov.uk/getamap
Ordnance Survey Get-a-map

★★★★★ UK

Get-a-Map is a free service from Ordnance Survey allowing you to print maps or copy them for use on your personal or business website, subject to their terms and conditions. You need to accept these before you you can proceed to the maps. You can zoom in from a map of Britain or search for a place name, postcode or grid reference. The maximum scale is 1:50,000 so although the Ordnance Survey detail is excellent for rural areas, it is less helpful for urban locations.

www.gazetteer.co.uk
Gazeteer of British Place Names

★★★★ UK

Come here for explanation of counties and administrative areas, plus an instant parish locator.

Maps: historical

For maps of individual counties, see the main listings on the GENUKI site (see p.29), and the sites selling antique and reproduction maps on pp.163-4.

www.ihr.sas.ac.uk/maps
Map History/History of Cartography

★★★★★ UK

A great set of resources for anyone interested in cartography, with sections devoted to map collecting, societies and important map collections. Under Links and Gateways you find Image Sites, which provides hundreds of annotated links to online maps, covering the whole world. These links are updated weekly.

www.old-maps.co.uk
Old-maps.co.uk

★★★★★ UK

The site provides access to Britain's most extensive digital historical map archive. A model of simplicity , this allows you to search old maps (usually 1882) for known place names or specific addresses, or by co-ordinates. Adjacent maps can be found via the directional arrows. In the enlarged view you then use the scroll bars to move around. You can also select a place name from the County Gazetteer. They have most editions of the historical Ordnance Survey maps, and you can compare various editions. Maps are provided either in printed form and posted to you, or produced electronically and emailed, the latter being cheaper. There is an Historical Maps email group to join.

Maps: historical London

In addition to the sites listed below, see also Gendocs (see p.62), which has an invaluable Victorian London A-Z Street Index, with over 61,000 references, telling you which date maps each entry will be found on.

www.bathspa.ac.uk/greenwood/imagemap.html
Greenwood's Map of London 1827

★★★★★ UK

With a slow internet connection it can take a long while to download the whole map, but the site works better if you do. There is an extensive list of place names, canals and future railway terminals and Thames features, such as docks and bridges. Clicking on any of these takes you straight to the part of the map that contains that feature.

www.perseus.tufts.edu
The Perseus Digital Library

★★★★★ UK

Click on London to find the Bolles Collection and then on London Maps for a large number of digitised maps of London, dating from 1600 to 1999, which are selected from a pull-down menu. These can all be compared to overlays of current-day roads and landmarks. Bolles' collection also contains many books and prints of London, and the aim is to be able to link through from the maps to relevant source text or illustrations. The online gazetteer is promised for many of the maps but was not available at the time of review.

www.ph.ucla.edu/epi/snow/1859map
Map of John Snow's London in 1859

★★★★★ UK

John Snow's (1813–58) was a famous epidemiologist and the map (Reynolds's Map of Modern London) illustrates Victorian London at the time he was working there. Searching the map online is a little complicated but the possibility of viewing quarter-mile sections is very useful.

http://booth.lse.ac.uk
Charles Booth Online Archive

★★★★ UK

Here you can browse (or buy) maps descriptive of London poverty 1898–99.

Medical terms

Causes of death as recorded on a death certificate can be obscure to the layman. Older certificates can also throw up archaic terms and rather vague-sounding causes. If you need help with interpretation, these sites will provide it.

www.paul_smith.doctors.org.uk/ArchaicMedical Terms.htm
Archaic Medical Terms

★★★★★ UK

An heroic one-man effort by Paul Smith, a British doctor who has provided an extremely thorough listing of all the archaic medical terminology you are likely to come across, together with very useful descriptions for the more common causes of death in the past, and meanings of some folk and slang terms. He also points out where terms we think we understand may have a different medical meaning, or different connotations when used in the past. If you can't find what you need on this site, or from any of the alternative reference sources Paul Smith recommends, you can email him with the details for a personal response. As well as the A-Z listing, there are guides to symbols, abbreviations, poisons, and epidemics, and an explanation of how deaths are registered in the UK, as well as the potential for errors to appear on a death certificate.

http://www.cancerweb.ncl.ac.uk/omd
The Online Medical Dictionary

★★★★ UK

A simple-to use and highly cross-referenced medical dictionary, the OMD contains contemporary terms as well as obscure ones (the subject listing suggests twelve terms relating to alchemy). As well as an alphabetical listing, there is a fast search facility or you can access the contents by subject area.

www.medterms.com
Medterms Medical Dictionary

★★★★★ UK

Part of the MedicineNet.com site, this A-Z has over 10,000 entries with short, accessible definitions.

Medieval

A good place to start, if you have managed to trace your ancestors back to the seventeenth century or earlier, is with the PRO leaflet Family History: Medieval and Early Modern Sources. This is available online at www.pro.gov.uk/leaflets/Riindex.asp.

www.medievalgenealogy.org.uk
Some notes on Medieval Genealogy

★★★★ UK

Site Map is the best way of accessing the riches here, or you can use the search box if you are looking for something specific on this authoritative and comprehensive site. The Introduction (found under Guide) provides a practical overview of the published works, records and other sources, and moves on to topics such as heraldry and herald's visitations, handwriting and language, calendar, chronology and dating. There is a full list of the City Livery companies, with links where they have websites. Chris Philips claims to be an amateur enthusiast, but this site is more rewarding than many professional ones.

www.odinscastle.org
Odin's Castle of Dreams and Legends

★★★★★ US

Don't let the fantasy trappings and cod-medieval greeting deter you from taking this site seriously. It is eccentric in presentation, but under sections with names like The Dungeon, the Gatehouse, The Buttery and The Privy there is the most staggering amount of information. Most of the Medieval History is contained in The Great Hall, and many other historical periods are covered.

www.netserf.org
Netserf: the Internet connection for Medieval Resources

★★★★ US

A great set of links covering all aspects of medieval history and culture. The law section is particular useful for genealogists, as is the Hypertext Medieval Glossary, with over 1500 archaic terms defined.

http://orb.rhodes.edu/Medieval_Terms.html
Guide to Medieval Terms

★★★★ US

JS Arkenberg edits this detailed alphabetical list of terms. Elsewhere on the ORB (Online Resource Book for Medieval Studies) site are myriad resources and links on every aspect of medieval history, religion and culture, both for the serious scholar and the nonspecialist.

Newsletters and online magazines

Many of the sites you will come across in your researches offer free email newsletters, and it may be worth signing up for a number of these to keep up to date with developments on sites of particular interest to you. The following is a selection of the most general-interest online genealogy journals. You will also find articles on the sites of the print magazines reviewed on p.162.

www.excite.co.uk/directory/Society/Genealogy/Magazines_and_E-zines
Excite Directory

★★★★★ UK

This is a useful shortcut to some of the online magazines mentioned below, with a handy preview button attached to each. Start here, then explore below.

www.ancestorsmagazine.co.uk
Ancestors Magazine

★★★★★ UK

Abstracts of articles from this excellent PRO publication can be read online, though to read them in full you need to subscribe. The 'In Previous Issues' link will help you decide whether to do so.

www.genuki.org.uk/news/
GENUKI Family History News

★★★★ UK

Rob Thompson's newsletter scores by being UK based, and providing one of the few sources of web and book reviews. From this page you can subscribe to the email newsletter and read previous newsletters in the archive. At the time of writing, the site had not been updated for some time. It is worth visiting the newsletter's original home at www.galethompson.freeserve.co.uk/familyhistory news.htm.

www.globalgazette.net
The Global Gazette Online Family History Magazine

★★★★ CAN

Owned by the Canadian genealogy publisher, Global Heritage Press, this weekly online magazine has particular relevance for anyone seeking Canadian connections, but the extensive archive of well-written articles has something to offer researchers wherever their roots are. Recent articles are listed on the homepage if you want to browse, or use the search box for specific queries.

www.rootsforum.com/newsletter
Eastman's Online Genealogy Newsletter

★★★★ US

This is the page to visit to subscribe to Dick Eastman's weekly newsletter which focuses on the technology available for use in researching family trees. It is a good place to look for reviews of software and data CD products. You can read the magazine online or opt to have it delivered to you by email each week. The archive is searchable by publication date or subject categories.

www.ancestry.com
Ancestry.com

★★★ US

Select Genealogy Research Help from the Homepage, under which is Free Genealogy Newsletters, for a list of this huge website's own products. Cyndi's List has a similar page, of course.

Newspapers and Journals

www.bodley.ox.ac.uk/ilej
Internet Library of Early Journals

★★★★★ UK

This is a digital library of 18th and 19th century journals, including at least twenty consecutive years of the Gentleman's Magazine, The Annual Register, Philosophical Transactions of the Royal Society, Notes and Queries, The Builder and Blackwood's Edinburgh Magazine. Other titles will be added and the much needed index and search facility extended to all the journals. Start with What is ILEJ and scroll down for a profile of each of the titles. If your ancestors were of a class to have contributed to or been written about in these journals it is a wonderful resource, and for the rest of us it is a great place to browse for period detail.

http://prodigi.bl.uk/nlcat
The Newspaper Library Catalogue

★★★★ UK

Part of the British Library website, from this page you can search the online catalogue of the UK's most comprehensive newspaper collection, which also has strong holdings of overseas newspapers, magazines and periodicals. For each entry you can see the dates between which the title was published. Click on Newspaper Library link at the top right of any page for background information on the collection and details of how to view publications at the repository's reading room in Colindale.

Photographs: dating

By far the most useful source for dating British photographs of people is the BBC's Guide to Victorian Studio Photographs, part of the site reviewed on p.29. There is a very lively email list of people waiting to help you if you send a message saying subscribe to VINTAGE-PHOTOS-L-request@rootsweb.com. For further details about subscribing to mailing lists, see p.38. Note: For help with locating images, whether of places or people, see Collage (p.77) or Buildings (p.133). Also, don't ignore Google, which offers an Images button above the normal search box. Using this will be likely to produce predominantly American images but you could well strike lucky. Similarly American is DeadFred at www.deadfred.com, the amusingly named people-image finder, an idea someone should launch here.

www.ajmorris.com/roots/photo/photo.htm
19th Century Photography

★★★★★ US

It is worth exploring all of the links here : History, Types, P&G (Photography and Genealogy) and Gallery; but the most useful section for estimating age is Dates, which considers all aspects of a photograph for the clues they give: details of the thickness and type of card, tax stamp, photographer imprint, portrait style, background and clothing styles, though these may obviously vary for countries outside the US. In P&G there is a useful discussion of methods of preservation, digital imaging and photos as records.

www.classyimage.com/
Classy Image

★★★★ US

Tips for Dating Old Photographs approaches dating with reference to the technologies used to produce the photograph, from Daguerrotypes to Wet Plate Prints. It presents quite technical information in an accessible way, though countries other than the US may have been slower or faster to adopt an evolving technology, and so the dates may be inaccurate.

www.familychronicle.com/dating.htm
Dating Old Photographs

★★★   US

A brief introduction to the subject is followed by a series of gallery pages offering photographs arranged by decade from 1840s to 1900s. The idea is to compare your photos with the poses and costumes of these images to get a feel for the period. Again, the usefulness for UK researchers is limited by this being an American site, therefore using American examples. You will also need to be careful about equating costume styles with a particular time period, since those lacking a high income would continue to make good use of their clothes many years after they supposedly went out of fashion.

www.heirlooms.com
Heirloom Search

★★★   UK

This is a straightforward site collecting family memorabilia, such as signed photographs, postcards and a few other documents. These are for sale.

www.victoriancostume.org.uk
Victorian Costume Site

★★★   UK

Head for the Site Map to navigate around this site. Unfortunately the images are arranged by the type of image (black and white drawings, colour drawings, and photographs from the Victorian Period), and then by

decade, so you may need to look in several different places to get a full view of a particular decade. It is frustrating that the Victorian photographs aren't dated, but this is still a useful site for getting a sense of the fashions in different parts of the nineteenth century. The links are also worth investigating.

Photographs: digital editing and preservation

Professional copying and restoration of old photographs is an expensive business, and with the wide availability of cheap scanners and photo-editing programs, it is increasingly viable to undertake your own digital editing. For good storage methods, see the Conservation by Design website on p.164.

www.city-gallery.com/digital/index.html
The Digital Album

★★★★   US

A great resource covering everything from building a digital album, choosing graphics formats, storage options, scanner tutorials, and preservation issues, and links to helpful scanning websites. At www.city-gallery.com/guide there are further resources on interpreting old photographs and downloadable charts, forms and a guide to help you in your family photo research, such as a printable family photo sheet, and Everything You Ever Wanted to Know about Your Family Photographs. These are downloadable as PDF files.

Tutorials

Many of the sites discussed in chapter 2 and elsewhere, particularly BBC, Society of Genealogists, GENUKI, PRO and FamilySearch, contain excellent introductory material in the form of articles or leaflets. If you are a beginner you shouldn't set foot online without looking at www.genuki.org.uk/gs, and particularly the Newbie section.

www.excite.co.uk/directory/Society/Genealogy/Resources/Tutorials
Excite Directory – Genealogy Tutorials

★★★★ ⓤ US

Here is a list of over 20 tutorials to choose from, though some are 'how to' sites rather than structured courses.

www.hellofresno.com/history/HowToWriteBios.html
How to Write a Biography

★★★ ⓤ US

Deb Christensen's single page of instructions for how to 'narrate' the history of family members is admirably simple and clear.

Weights and Measures

www.omnis.demon.co.uk
The Foot Rule

★★★★ UK

If you need to know how many pounds a truss of straw, or a tod of wool, weighs, check out the Old English Commodity Measures table on the Foot Rule site. There are many other conversions you can make on this site using the Units Calculator, and more tables such as capacities and book sizes.

http://privatewww.essex.ac.uk/~alan/family/N-Units.html
Weights and Measures

★★★★ UK

Alan Stanier provides a simple table showing the decimal equivalents of pounds, shillings, pence, florins and guineas and other archaic coins. It then goes on to interpret old linear measures such as hands, feet, rods, poles and perches; and capacity measures such as bushels and hogsheads. Useful dates such as Lady Day and Michaelmas Day are given, and the regnal years of British monarchs since William I. Click on the link for Relative Value of Sums of Money, which provides tables such as the Daily Money Wage Rates of Building Craftsmen and Labourers in Southern England 1264-1954.

http://home.clara.net/brianp/index.html
English Weights and Measures

★★★★ UK

Partly aimed at collectors, this is nevertheless a good source of basic conversion information.

Have you registered for **free updates?**

log on to

www.thegoodweguide.co.uk

Chapter 9

buying goods and services online

Many people are still reluctant to make purchases on the internet, scared off by rumours of credit-card fraud. But anyone who has experienced the excellent and reliable service of a company such as Amazon will probably be converted to its advantages. When trying to track down specialist items such as genealogy supplies, the convenience of this way of shopping becomes quickly apparent. Certainly you should not be put off from ordering by the credit-card issue. Most sites offer other methods of payment and if you stick to the following guidelines you should be safe:

• Never give your credit card details to a site that doesn't have a secure server. There should be a locked padlock in the bottom left corner before you type in your details, and the web address should change from http:// to https:// when you've been transferred to a secure server.

• Look out for Which? Webtrader sites. These have all been vetted for secure transactions, privacy policies and consumer guarantees. But not all sites that haven't entered the scheme are necessarily rogue sites – use your judgement and, if in doubt, don't buy.

• Never, ever, put your credit card details in an email – they are not secure and can be intercepted. Better to telephone or fax.

• Don't trade with sites that don't give full contact details, including a telephone and street address, plus details of how they deal with returns.

If you follow the guidelines, buying on the internet need not be any more risky than handing over your credit card in a shop or restaurant, or over the phone.

You should not necessarily be put off by the thought of ordering from abroad. There is currently no VAT charged on books, and carriage costs can be surprisingly reasonable, especially if you are not in a hurry and can opt for surface mail in the case of heavy items. Lighter books travel quickly and inexpensively anyway. Certainly, if the book you want is rare due to a small print-run, out of print or difficult to find, it may be worth paying to obtain it from abroad.

In the case of second-hand or antiquarian books, again it may be worth looking overseas. For example, a rare history of an English county that would be extremely relevant (and consequently expensive) if sold at home might be languishing on the shelves of a bookseller abroad, under-appreciated and under-priced.

Of course it is not just books that you can shop for online. This chapter covers software, data CDs, magazines and journals, microfiche and film readers, maps and every sort of genealogy supply you can think of.

General Supplies

Deciding which categories to put sites into has proved particularly difficult in this chapter, as there is considerable overlap. The following sites supply more than one type of aid for your genealogical research, so they could equally well be listed under software, data CDs, books or microfiche, and probably some others as well.

www.genfair.com
GENfair

Overall rating: ★★★★			
Classification:	Ecommerce	Readability:	★★★★
Updating:	Daily	Content:	★★★★
Navigation:	★★★★★	Speed:	★★★★★

UK

Laid out so that users can approach it as if visiting a trade fair, this website contains a wide range of products for purchase that may help the family and local historian. The products are offered by over 85 different 'stands', each representing a small enterprise or society. The centralised shopping basket system allow you to buy from any of them with a single payment. Click on the Shop at GENfair button at the bottom of the page to enter.

SPECIAL FEATURES

Main Hall indexes all the stands, with a particularly good list of Family History Societies, every one with a link to its online presence. Other useful websites are assembled under the title Ancestry Arcade.

Classified Guide directs you to stands by subject listing, so if you know you are looking for census materials or guides for beginners, you don't have to wade through every stand to find them. The range of products here is really very comprehensive, and like most fairs, if you browse the stands you will find things you didn't even know you needed.

UK Family History Page offers links to the top ten internet sites for UK genealogy.

Update introduces new items for sale, or stands that are newcomers to GENfair, which is useful for regular users.

Location Finder allows you to click on a map of the UK or Ireland (no contributors from the latter yet) and find a list of Family History Societies county by county.

As they themselves say, a one-stop shop for all your genealogy needs. Note: At the time of this revision GENfair had just announced its acquisition by the Federation of History Societies Publications Ltd. There is currently no web presence, until the location for the new GENfair website is decided.

www.genealogy.demon.co.uk
S & N Genealogy Supplies

Overall rating: ★ ★ ★ ★ ★

Classification:	Ecommerce	Readability:	★ ★ ★ ★
Updating:	Daily	Content:	★ ★ ★ ★
Navigation:	★ ★ ★ ★	Speed:	★ ★ ★ ★

UK 🛈

This is a very haphazard site, with lots of out-of-date links, and parallel sites, but the range of products stocked makes it a must-visit destination for the serious researcher. They provide computer software, books, charts and CD data disks. Moreover, S & N offer ongoing support to their customers, without charging premium telephone rates.

From the homepage you are faced with three links, one telling you to 'Click here to read about...', another offering the British Data Archive, and a third linking to a Duplicate Site. Choosing the first link does actually transfer you to a different URL. There are numerous links with no particular hierarchy so just scroll and browse on any that take your fancy.

They also run training courses for users of Family Tree Maker and Generations Grande Suite, which you can make use of if you can get to Salisbury, where they are based.

SPECIAL FEATURES

London Census is where you can read about the first fruits of S&N's initiative to digitise images of census returns and distribute them on sets of CDs and DVDs. London 1891 was the first such project, and plans are in progress to extend this to other counties and census years. Very worthwhile.

CD Data Discs is a particularly strong category, with a wide selection of products, some of which are exclusive to S&N, others more widely available. The selection includes parish registers, trade directories, monumental inscriptions, criminal registers, gazetteers and an interactive Ordnance Survey atlas.

Genealogy Books and Aids offers a useful list of books and booklets as well as, at the bottom of that page, The Ancestral Oak, an attractive chart on which to present six generations of your family tree.

Why Buy from S & N? with its link to Customer Comments should convince you of the efficiency of the service.

Genealogy Events is a convenient shortcut to finding out if there are any forthcoming events in your area.

Essential port-of-call if you need to order computer software, books, data CDs or accessories for genealogy purposes.

www.twrcomputing.freeserve.co.uk
TWR Computing

Overall rating: ★ ★ ★ ★ ★

Classification:	Software	Readability:	★ ★ ★ ★
Updating:	Regularly	Content:	★ ★ ★ ★
Navigation:	★ ★ ★ ★ ★	Speed:	★ ★ ★ ★ ★

UK 🔒

This is Trevor Rix's Genealogy and Family History software supplies service, which offers unlimited ongoing customer support. Computers and computer programs for other applications are sold too, all with a lowest price guarantee. It is their first-rate personal customer service that sets this organisation apart. Rix has years of experience of supplying low-cost computer systems for family historians, put together to your exact specification. They will also pre-install the software programs so even an inexperienced user can get up and running quickly. This service is not well advertised on the site, but is explained in About (accessible from the homepage), or call or email them to discuss your requirements. The site itself is very straightforward with new products accessible from the arrival page.

SPECIAL FEATURES

Family History and Genealogy Software Click here to access a list of products, first of software programs and then of Data CDs. Secure online ordering is available, as well as other payment methods.

Programs offers the latest versions of the main family history programs, as well as more specialist utilities, such as Folio Views, which allows Mac users to view the LDS 1881 census CDs.

Data CDs is a growing selection. They carry the S&N census CDs, as well as a range that usually comes bundled with

Family Tree Maker, which includes some interesting Irish records, such as Tithe Applotment Books, Source Records 1500-1800, Griffiths Valuation of Ireland Index, and an Index of Irish Wills 1484-1858.

A reliable and knowledgeable software and hardware supplier, open from 8am to 10pm seven days a week, with same day despatch and an emphasis on customer service.

www.jenlibrary.u-net.com
The Family History Shop and Library

Overall rating: ★ ★ ★			
Classification:	Books	**Readability:**	★ ★ ★ ★
Updating:	Regularly	**Content:**	★ ★ ★
Navigation:	★ ★ ★	**Speed:**	★ ★ ★

UK

Jenifer Edmonds set up this service in 1992, when she opened a bricks and mortar shop in Norwich. The Local History & Genealogy Library soon followed.

SPECIAL FEATURES

The homepage offers links to either the Shop or the Library Service. There is a good list of titles available from the Shop, including books, microfiche, maps and other articles. The actual Library in Norwich can be used at a rate of £2.00 per hour. Alternatively you can request printouts of documents, at a rate of £2.00 per surname per index and 10p per sheet. You can communicate by post, telephone or email, and commission either research or courier service delivery of BDM certificates and copies of census entries.

There is no online ordering facility but if you want to pay by credit card, the Family History Shop may in due course continue to be hosted by GENfair (see p.148).

The research emphasis is on Norfolk and Suffolk but there are other resources here of good general interest.

Books

Your first choice for buying genealogy books online may be sites listed elsewhere in this book. If you are a regular Amazon user and know what you're looking for, they can supply most books that are in print (and some which are not). The Society of Genealogists (see. p.41) and the PRO (p.44) both have online bookshops selling their own publications. And some of the companies listed in General Supplies, particular S&N, have very useful booklists. For rarer items, see the list of Antiquarian booksellers on p.154.

www.amazon.co.uk			
Amazon			
Overall rating: ★ ★ ★ ★ ★			
Classification:	Books	Readability:	★ ★ ★ ★ ★
Updating:	Regularly	Content:	★ ★ ★ ★ ★
Navigation:	★ ★ ★ ★ ★	Speed:	★ ★ ★ ★ ★
UK 🔒			

Though not specifically for genealogists, we find it impossible to fault this site. The breadth of titles, ease and flexibility of its ordering system, efficient search facility, low prices and excellent service, mean there is little more that you could ask for. To access the genealogy titles, either type Genealogy in the Quicksearch box, or go to History, Cultural History, Genealogy. For specialist publications you may wait longer than going directly to specialist suppliers, but titles are usually delivered well within the long order times indicated.

www.ukgenealogy.co.uk/genbooks/main.htm			
UK GenBooks			
Overall rating: ★ ★ ★ ★			
Classification:	Books	Readability:	★ ★ ★ ★
Updating:	Weekly	Content:	★ ★ ★ ★
Navigation:	★ ★ ★ ★	Speed:	★ ★ ★ ★ ★
UK 🔒			

Linked to Amazon.co.uk and Amazon.com, through whom any actual ordering and despatch are done, this website specialises in genealogy titles in print.

SPECIAL FEATURES

Books are sorted according to the following links: Census Returns, Parish Registers, Public Record Office, Gibson Guides, McLaughlin Guides and New to Family History. If Gibson and McLaughlin are unfamiliar names to you, the best route to seeing what these guides cover is to click on their links in the homepage index box, which will give a category list before you start consulting individual titles.

Below the brown index links is a yellow box offering the names of other genealogy booksellers, to which links are also available. On the occasion tested two of these websites were unavailable, one of them being **Booth Books**, which is the link to the book 'town' of Hay-on-Wye. Another book town has now been established in Galloway in Scotland, and the link to that is **GC Books**.

Lesley Aitchison specialises in maps, documents and ephemera, while **Ambra Books** deals with antiquarian and secondhand books relating to Gloucestershire, Wiltshire and counties west. **Stuart Raymond** is another general genealogy specialist selling in-print books.

Incidentally, well towards the bottom of this homepage is a search box linked to Amazon.co.uk where you can try to locate a book via keywords rather than the full title.

This is an excellent route to sifting out genealogy titles, and online ordering is straightforward, with all the advantages of the Amazon system.

www.hawgood.co.uk
David and Barbara Hawgood

★★★★ UK

David Hawgood, sometimes in conjunction with Peter Christian, has written a number of small books about genealogy on the internet. The main object here is to introduce the various titles by David Hawgood that are currently in print and direct you to the various places where they are available. One of his recent titles, GENUKI – UK & Ireland Genealogy on the Internet, is available from the homepage in an online form and is a very clear and helpful guide to negotiating the vast resources that GENUKI (see p. 29) contains. The site is also worth a visit for the excellent online articles and links to other sites.

Antiquarian Booksellers

The following are all antiquarian or second-hand book dealers, some with UK-specific options. They all use a system either the same as, or similar to, Amazon, so it does not seem necessary to describe the navigation of each website individually.

Abebooks.com
www.abebooks.com

Alibris
www.alibris.com

Bibliofind
www.bibliofind.com

Biblion
www.biblion.co.uk

Blackwell's Rare Books
http://rarebooks.blackwell.co.uk

Book Avenue
www.bookavenue.com

Ambra Books
www.localhistory.co.uk/ambra

Add ALL
www.addall.com
This site is an umbrella search facility that will sift through many of the above sites.

World Book Dealers
www.worldbookdealers.com
A portal for a number of smaller antiquarian and second-hand dealers, all grouped under this one website.

Amazon
www.amazon.com and www.amazon.co.uk
Both of the Amazon sites have in-print and older books under a specialist genealogy heading.

Roy Davids Ltd
www.roydavids.com
Specialist dealer in manuscripts, letters, archives and portraits, a dangerously enticing place in which to look for that very special present!

Paper Antiques
www.paperantiques.co.uk/dealerspages.htm
An umbrella for a number of dealers in collectibles, ephemera and all sorts of paper memorabilia, including photographs, postcards and cigarette cards.

Reynolds Collectors World
www.reynolds-s-a.freeserve.co.uk
Click on the Reynolds Collectors' World link for a website that specialises in early postcards and other ephemera.

Chapel Books
www.chapelbooks.co.uk
Chapel Books specialise in books and documents for genealogists and local historians, searchable by county, and a selection of Family Histories.

John Townsend
www.johntownsend.demon.co.uk
John Townsend is an antiquarian bookseller specialising in Genealogy, British Topography and Local History.

Kingfisher Book Service
www.kingfisher-books.co.uk
Kingfisher books will undertake a free book-search for you, and provides a message board where you can post details of books you are seeking on a 'Wants List'.

Software and Data

From the following sites you can purchase latest versions of specialist genealogy programs (see also p. 158-60). As many of these are widely available, it is worth comparing prices on a number of sites (including non-specialist software suppliers) before buying.

As the costs of scanning and producing CDs has plummeted, there has been a proliferation of suppliers of specialist genealogical data, such as trade directories and parish records, that previously you would have needed to visit local records offices to access. Microfiche has lost some ground as the genealogists' favourite format because of the rise of CDs. Most computers now come supplied with CD-rom drives. But fiche is cheap and light, easy to store, and is still the preferred form if you are borrowing records from an LDS Family History Centre, so don't write it off yet!.

In addition on the sites listed in this section, you should also check out the following sites reviewed elsewhere, which have very broad stock:

Society of Genealogists
www.sog.org.uk

S&N
www.genealogy.demon.co.uk

TWR Computing
www.twrcomputing.freeserve.co.uk

LDS
www.lds.org.uk/genealogy/software.htm

www.backtoroots.co.uk
Back to Roots (UK) Ltd

Overall rating: ★ ★ ★ ★			
Classification:	Software	Readability:	★ ★ ★
Updating:	Regularly	Content:	★ ★ ★
Navigation:	★ ★ ★ ★ ★	Speed:	★ ★ ★ ★ ★

UK

A straightforward site with a lot of useful products tucked away here.

SPECIAL FEATURES

Software leads you to a broad range of top genealogy programs, plus a range of Family Tree Maker Data CDs, which include a good number of Irish records.

Directories The list includes street and trade directories for most counties.

Census and Misc As well as stocking S&N's 1891 CDs, there are some fairly rare early census datasets available here.

Criminal Register Available on disk, CD-rom and fiche, the full range of Stuart Tamblin's lists of criminals between 1805 and 1892 in the series of registers now held as Series HO 27 at the Public Record Office at Kew. Full information from the registers is provided: names, aliases, court, offence, and sentence/acquittal.

Militia Musters Mostly covering the period 1781-83, these discs provide indexes and details of the men who served, culled from a wide range of regiments and counties.

Certificate Binder This button leads you to a range of certificate binders, acid-free stationery, recording aids for censuses, parish registers and tree blanks. It will also lead you to a list of the very-well regarded short books by Colin Chapman and Eve McLaughlin.

Orders/Enquiry   At the time of writing, secure online ordering was in development. Until it arrives an online form allows you to place an order or submit an enquiry, but we recommend phoning or faxing credit-card details rather than using the email form, which is not secure.

Family History Fairs Fairs at which Back to Roots is exhibiting.

Links A small but useful set of links to suppliers of specialist goods and services such as maps for family historians, and genealogy printers that can print out at up to A0 size sheets from genealogical programmes.

An excellent source for difficult-to-track down data and products.

www.rod-neep.co.uk
Rod Neep Books/The Archive CD Books Project

Overall rating: ★ ★ ★ ★

Classification:	CD-Rom	Readability:	★ ★ ★ ★
Updating:	Regularly	Content:	★ ★ ★ ★ ★
Navigation:	★ ★ ★ ★ ★	Speed:	★ ★ ★ ★ ★

UK 🔒

The Archive CD Books Project scans and restores rare old books, documents and maps and distributes them on CDs. Their holdings cover directories such as Pigot's and Kelly's, gazetteers, church records, history and topography, marriage licences and bonds, war records and much more. The average price of a CD is £8.50 plus postage and packing. The site is not constructed in a way to endear itself to the user, but the project itself is so worthwhile, and the books such a boon to family historians, that it is worth persevering.

Online Catalogue and Ordering   Once you've selected this option, it is worth following their own advice to use the site map to navigate, as this provides you with a manageable list of available products ordered by county, and type of resource. But scroll down the page to find the link to original old books for sale and details of how to sponsor a book. Online ordering is secure, and the newsgroups are full of people praising their service and products.

The CDs contain digitised images of the original pages either in HTML format, which you can read in your browser, or as PDF files, for which you need Adobe Acrobat Reader (see p.22). The universal nature of these formats means that they can be used on Apple Macs or Linux computers as well as Windows-based operating systems.

About the Project and **Questions & Support** are well worth reading to help you appreciate the value of this project, which has a commitment to preservation alongside its commercial aims.

Sponsor a Book If you pay £25 towards the cost of restoring an original book, you will be entitled to free CDs and a permanent 15% discount. After scanning, the books are professionally rebound and donated to a library or record office.

A great idea that you will enjoy supporting, and a great way to get your hands on rare trade directories.

Software programs

Suppliers of a range of genealogy software have been listed elsewhere (see pp.148-51 and 155). The sites listed here are those provided by the software developers themselves, and are worth consulting for detailed information on demos, latest versions and upgrades. Some also supply online support, FAQs and even dedicated areas for uploading your family trees to the web. Worth perusing then to get a sense of the the benefits of a programme before you buy, though you may get better deals and more UK specific extras by buying from UK genealogy specialists such as S&N, TWR and the SoG.

The selection here is based on an evaluation of the supporting website and does not necessarily imply that these are the best programs for you to buy. For further help on choosing a genealogy program, see the article on http://thegoodwebguide.co.uk/chan_gene or Bill Mumford's comparative guide at www.mumford.ab.ca/reportcard. You should also check the Genealogy Shoppers Guide on www.genealogyforum.rootsweb.com/store/softwarest.htm

Finally, for what the future may offer see George G. Morgan's article 'Genealogical Software: The Next Generation', which you will find at www.ancestry.com/library/view/gencomp/1611asp.

www.familytreemaker.com
Family Tree Maker

★★★★★ US 🔒

As the introduction says, this is America's number one selling family tree program. You can buy various packages of the same basic program, some of which include data CDs, subscriptions to Genealogy.com and other online data sources. The program entitles you to upload your data to the Family Tree Maker site, which is integrated with Genealogy.com, though it is not possible to upload them onto your website, which many other programs do allow you to do. However, it is incredibly sophisticated, yet by all accounts exceptionally easy to use, and Family Tree Maker (now in Version 10) is state-of-the-art when it comes to organising your own family history records. A useful tip may be to look at this product on Amazon (using the co.uk suffix) and read the customer reviews, which make it very clear that the basic programme for storing your genealogical data is excellent but the accompanying software is of little relevance unless you are American.

www.legacyfamilytree.com
Legacy Family Tree Genealogy Software

★★★★★ US 🔒

At the time of writing you can download the Legacy 4.0 version of this well-respected program for free (apart from the telephone costs for the time it takes to download, which can be considerable). Alternatively you can pay for the Deluxe edition, which comes with extra features such as the ability to compare two files for duplicates before you merge them, a relationship calculator, and the ability to produce reports as PDF files, so they can be easily emailed and viewed by anyone who doesn't have a genealogy program.

www.leisterpro.com
Reunion

★★★★★ US

Apple Mac users will search in vain for bargain-price genealogy programmes. For fully-featured family history software, Reunion, which retails at around £80, is the only choice. The consolation is that it is an excellent and easy-to-use programme. From the site you can download a demo, sign up for a free daily email digest, link to the pages of other Reunion users, contact their technical support, and find out where you can buy it.

www.bkwin.com
Brother's Keeper Homepage

★★★★ US

Widely respected as one of the best software applications for storing your family history data, Brother's Keeper can be accessed and viewed here online. You can't download the entire program without paying but the chance to have a good look at its capabilities before committing yourself is useful, as is the ability to get going right away, without needing to go to the shops or wait for a delivery.

www.familysearch.com
Personal Ancestral File at Family Search

★★★★ US

From the homepage, click on Order/Download Products, then hit Software Downloads – Free. As the heading suggests, you can download various editions of the Personal Ancestral File (PAF) without payment. If you are still using an MS Dos or Windows 3.1 on an older computer, the older verions of PAF2 will be a very welcome option. There is also a Mac version available. If you decide to use this program, you might also want to go to www.saintclair.org/paf/ where there is plenty of information for PAF users and links to other sites that provide help. If you don't want to spend the time downloading the program from the web, which can be time-consuming and cause problems if your ISP logs you out after a fixed amount of time, you can purchase the PAF very cheaply, along with other LDS products such as the 1881 census and the BVRI, and PAF Companion, which allows you to you to print more complex charts and reports, from www.lds.org.uk (see p.37).

www.familyorigins.com
Family Origins Genealogy Software

★★★★ US

Family Origins was another fully-featured program with regular upgrades, but it has now been absorbed by Family Tree Maker. This page offers some software to make the transfer as painless as possible.

www.clooz.com
Clooz

★★★★ US

Not a standard genealogy program, Clooz describes itself as an electronic filing cabinet that assists you with search and retrieval of important facts you have found during the ancestor hunt (and goodness knows, that must beat all the notes written on backs of envelopes and never retrieved!). You can try out a demo from this site, which is very worthwhile as it is difficult to explain the advantages of this program. There's also a lengthy review on site which will help you decide if it could be of use to you.

http://members.aol.com/pandssmith/Custodian.htm
Custodian II for Family Historians

★★★★ UK

Created specifically for UK researchers, Custodian is not a family tree program, but a series of databases with pre-defined forms designed to store genealogical information. Useful for people who are amassing a lot of information, such as a one-name study. Because it has been built to accommodate the formats of common sources such as birth and marriage certificates, and IGI data, the program requires little customisation, and yet offers a great deal of flexibility in producing reports and storing data. A slideshow on the site will run you through the use and advantages of this utility.

www.ourtimelines.com
Our Timelines

★★★ US

This is a little bit of fun, but it is American so you may want to edit it a bit. Basically, the idea is that you can use this program to create your own timeline, fitting your own family landmarks into history at large.

www.oldfashionedclipart.com
J.O.D's Old Fashioned B&W Clip Art Collection

★★★★★ US

This is a wondrous collection of out-of-copyright graphics available for 'pasting' into your own family history pages (free of charge provided not for commercial purposes). Right mouse click on an image and you can then 'save picture as...' All J. O'Donovan asks is that you acknowledge his website if you use these images in a webpage.

Others to consider include:

www.genealogy.demon.co.uk/CFTWin.htm
Cumberland Tree V2
www.genealogy.demon.co.uk/corel.htm
Corel Family Tree Suite and Publisher
www.twrcomputing.freeserve.co.uk/tmg.htm
The Master Genealogist

Fiche and Film Readers

If you are going to pursue serious home-based researches in detail, a microfiche reader is invaluable, and the following are reliable suppliers, who also offer other specialist equipment and services.

---

www.marathon-microfilm-cdrom.co.uk
Marathon Microfilming Ltd

★★★　　US

The Marathon Microfilming homepage is reasonably quick to load. In addition to microfiche readers, Marathon offer a CD duplication service, which is useful if you want to distribute the fruits of your own researches, as it is much more cost effective than producing books or booklets. They will also scan original documents and output to microfiche or CD-roms. The business does not list prices online, presumably because they change regularly, so you have to telephone or email to obtain price lists. As a guideline, though, a microfiche reader will cost £150-£250, and they sometimes have reconditioned readers in stock.

---

http://www.mw-microfilm.co.uk
MW Microfilm Supplies

★★★　　UK

The links at the bottom of the homepage are slow to load, and may not even be visible on some browsers or Macs. However, MW are among the principal suppliers of fiche readers, printers, lamps, binders and other accessories. No prices are listed, though there are pictures and details of their range of readers, so you have to telephone or email for a price list.

---

www.intercomUK.com
Intercom

★★★　　UK

The pulsing buttons and moving text on this site can leave you feeling a bit nauseous, but the specialist services on offer here may be worth the effort. Intercom offer scanning services and can output to microfilm or fiche directly from digital files, as well as original documents. They stock a range of equipment for reading, printing and storing microform data, including some high spec readers. As with the other suppliers, you will need ultimately to contact them by conventional means if you wish to make a purchase, although some prices are given on site.

Magazines

Included in this section are only magazines for which you need a paid subscription.

In addition to the titles reviewed here, there are many other journals produced by various genealogical societies and distributed as part of their membership packages. See, for example, the Society of Genealogists, which publishes The Genealogists' Magazine and Computers in Genealogy, back issues of which can be ordered from their website at www.sog.org.uk. The Federation of Family History Societies (www.ffhs.org.uk) publishes Family History News and Digest.

If you want to read general articles about family history or genealogy, there are many good newsletters that you can receive by email, and which are usually free (see p.142).

www.ancestorsmagazine.co.uk
Ancestors

★★★★★ UK £ 🔒

The Family History magazine of the Public Record Office, this new bi-monthly magazine is a welcome addition to this rapidly expanding market, because it combines a rigorous approach with an accessible style, and a standard of production values that puts most of the supposedly commercial offerings to shame. From the site you can view the contents of previous issues and read a selection of features on the site to help you decide if it's for you. You can subscribe online, and although it is not cheap it represents good value. See also p.142.

www.family-tree.co.uk
ABM Publishing Ltd

★★★★★ UK £ 🔒

ABM are the publishers of two of the most popular family history magazines, Family Tree Magazine, and the more introductory Practical Family History. You can find details of the articles in the current editions of each title by clicking on the front covers displayed on the homepage. Family Tree Resources allows you to interrogate back issues of the magazine, at which point you may want to go to the Online Shop (in the left-of-page index), to buy either a specified back issue, or something from their very large and very useful list of books.

www.everton.com
Everton Publishers

★★★★★ US R

This is the online presence of one of the oldest established genealogy magazines, Everton's Genealogical Helper, founded in 1947 and now transformed into Family History Magazine. As a US publication, not everything is relevant to non-American researchers, but there is plenty here to investigate nonetheless. The magazine is sometimes available in UK newsagents and bookshops. To access much of the information you need to register, and you can also sign up for a free Family History Newsline, an email service that promises tips and information about genealogy. Once registered you can search the online Bureau of Missing Ancestors, read a selection of articles from past issues, take the 5 steps to Research online course, which has levels for beginners, Experienced researchers and Advanced. A good selection of free forms can be downloaded.

www.familychronicle.com
Family Chronicle

★★★★ US

Although published in America, Family Chronicle is a very well-produced magazine, with lots of articles that are relevent to non-US family historians. There is a good selection of articles available to sample online.

Maps

www.alangodfreymaps.co.uk
Old Ordnance Survey Maps

★★★★★ UK

Specialising in reprints of Victorian Ordnance Survey Maps, Alan Godfrey's maps are highly detailed, and at about 14 inches to the mile, they show individual houses, railway tracks, factories, churches, and so on. Each map also includes historical notes on the areas, and many also include extracts from contemporary directories such as Kelly's and Pigot's. The maps cost £2.10 each plus 50p per order postage. You need to phone to give credit card details or send a cheque, and the site lists various outlets where you can view or buy the maps. The company has built up a reputation for personal service and fast despatch. Highly recommended.

www.village-atlas.com
The Village Atlas and Hampden Maps

★★★★★ UK

The Village Atlas series of A3 maps, on a scale of 2 inches to a mile, allow comparisons to be made of an area from the early-nineteenth to early-twentieth century. For £7 you receive three maps spanning a period of 50-90 years depending on the region. They are also building a range of county maps and town plans. Secure online ordering is available via Worldpay, and orders are despatched within three working days. Enquiries are dealt with promptly by email though no phone number is given. A search facility would be a welcome addition.

www.allmappedout.com
All Mapped Out

★★★★★ UK

This is an attractive and well-ordered site from another specialist in historical Ordnance Survey maps. All Mapped Out carry an archive of over 20,000 maps from the early-nineteenth century to the 1930s, on a variety of scales. They cover all English and Welsh counties, and most of Ireland. There are good descriptions with pictures of the different series available, though you can't order online. In any case the maps are printed off to order, so it is important to contact them by phone or email so they can advise you on which maps would best suit your needs. Each map costs £13 plus postage and packing.

www.antiqueprints.com
Steve Bartrick Antique Prints and Maps

★★★★★ UK

A simple site with a good selection of old and antique maps and prints, each of which is displayed on the site. Wonderful presents for the family historian looking to put some flesh on the bones.

Conservation

www.conservation-by-design.co.uk
Conservation By Design

★★★★ UK

Armed with a royal warrant, Conservation by Design offers archival-quality boxes, transparent album pages and acid-free storage materials. They can supply everything you need if you are undertaking restoration jobs as well.

Courses

The following are all professionally recognised bodies running courses in genealogy. A search in Google may well produce others run by individuals calling themselves 'professional genealogists' and, while these may be excellent, you should first check what qualifications they have before parting with your money.

www.sog.org.uk/events
Society of Genealogists

★★★★★ UK

The Society of Genealogists run a range of courses, lectures and workshops, available to non-members, from afternoon events to 15-week courses for genealogists of all levels, mostly held at the Society's building or other London venues. Booking forms are avalable in PDF format online.

www.ihgs.ac.uk
Institute of Heraldic and Genealogical Studies

★★★★★ UK

The IHGS is an independent educational charitable trust providing courses and facilities for people wishing to acquire skills in family history research. Their qualifications are widely recognised as the leading ones for professional genealogists, although they also offer courses from beginner level, through evening and day classes, full-time courses and residential courses held at universities and other institutions around the country. They are based in Canterbury but for those who cannot attend in person, there is a correspondence course that can lead to the Institute's Certificate in Genealogy.

www.tall.ox.ac.uk/localhistory
Advanced Diploma in Local History

★★★★★ UK

Oxford University Department for Continuing Education offers an Advanced Diploma in Local History via the internet, with the full support of a personal tutor. Despite the course title, the course claims to be aimed at people undertaking their own research into family history, as well as local history.

www.bbk.ac.uk
Birkbeck, University of London

★★★★★ UK

Birkbeck is one of the colleges of the University of London, and specialises in part-time courses for mature students. They offer a certificate and a diploma in Genealogy. To find details of the course follow the links to Courses, Faculty of Continuing Education Prospectus, History and Genealogy. At the bottom of that page you will find two courses for genealogists, an Introduction and Further Sources. Both include a visit to the Family Records Centre. The site also lists details of accredited courses held at other centres, mostly in the home counties.

Chapter 10

research services

Most of the websites in this chapter do not restrict themselves to the provision of research services. Some offer numerous links to further genealogical information, while others sell publications or software. But the sites featured here all provide specific, one-to-one assistance.

This assistance is offered in two ways. There are many individuals and a few organisations who will carry out genealogical research on your behalf. Usually you have to pay for this help, though quite often an assessment of the likelihood of any success will be given first, with an estimate of cost. In these cases, you do not have to commit yourself to paying until you decide whether it will be worthwhile. You can often arrange to pay in instalments or agree to pay in the first instance up to an agreed limit and only authorise further payments later. Factors that will influence your decision will be related either to the difficulty of finding out the information for yourself, or to the cost in time and possibly in travel and accommodation costs that

would be incurred if you carried out the same research yourself. Against this background the fees often seem very moderate.

The importance of assuring yourself of the professional credentials of anyone you employ to do this sort of work cannot be over-stressed. There are many highly skilled, highly professional researchers out there ready to help you. There are also untrained amateurs trying to jump on what they see as a gravy-train.

The other sort of service that is available here is record-collecting and transmitting, usually by post but sometimes by email, in cases where you have already identified the documents you want and simply need someone else to pick them up and send them on to you. Companies or individuals who specialise in particular types of records can often offer very competitive prices and quick turnarounds.

www.achievements.co.uk
Achievements of Canterbury

Overall rating: ★ ★ ★ ★ ★			
Classification: Heraldry		**Readability:**	★ ★ ★ ★
Updating: Occasionally		**Content:**	★ ★ ★ ★
Navigation: ★ ★ ★ ★		**Speed:**	★ ★ ★ ★

UK R

Based in Canterbury, Achievements was established some 40 years ago, making it the oldest genealogical research organisation of its kind. It is linked with the Institute of Heraldic and Genealogical Studies (see p.170), whose work it supports, and all its researchers are fully IHGS trained. For a fee, Achievements will help you with anything from sorting out a sticky patch in your research to creating an entire pedigree. Their researchers have been featured in recent television programmes about genealogy, such as BBC2's Blood Ties and Channel 4's Extraordinary Ancestors.

SPECIAL FEATURES

Services not only includes tracing ancestors, but also such tasks as establishing the right to bear a Coat of Arms, tracing missing heirs or relatives, transcribing or translating old handwriting, researching the history of your house or locality, and even advising on the purchase of lordships and baronies. They will organise tours for overseas visitors to show them the places where their ancestors lived. Achievements can provide a fully 'scrivened' family tree (that is, which includes calligraphic script, handmade paper, heraldic artwork) or create for you an individual Family History book. They will also undertake research to reunite adopted children with their natural parents and family.

Trace your Ancestors Links from the homepage to a series of Request A Quote forms for you to outline the nature of your research enquiry and to supply as much detail as possible. A quotation for the work is then returned by email. As it may take more than one sitting to assemble all the information you need, you can register to set up an account so that you can retrieve the details you entered in a previous session.

Visit Achievements gives details of the Heraldry Centre in Northgate, Canterbury, where you can arrange a consultation if your research has run aground. Here they will also organise special tours, principally for visitors from abroad, going to the villages, churches and possibly even the homes where ancestors lived.

Links to other sites includes Search and Unite, run by David Lewin in London and Margret Chatwin in Munich, whose aim is to find and reunite people who became separated during the Second World War (at a rate of £10 per hour) and to undertake property claims in the Czech Republic, which they do on a contingency basis.

The long-established and professionally staffed nature of this research organisation makes it a reliable choice for those needing some support in taking their research forward.

AGRA has changed its name from The Association of Genealogists and Record Agents to The Association of Genealogists and Researchers in Archives. Founded in 1968 to promote expertise in the fields of genealogy, heraldry and record searching, AGRA lists only those researchers who meet specified standards of competence and comply with AGRA's own Code of Practice. By employing any AGRA member to help you in your research, therefore, you are guaranteed a certain level of professionalism. The price you pay is agreed with the researcher, who will either estimate for a defined task or will agree an expenditure limit where the task is more open-ended.

SPECIAL FEATURES

List of Members Available for Commission This section explains the distinction between genealogists, who have proven skills to create pedigrees, and a researcher in archives, who will undertake a wide variety of historical research, including the gathering of genealogical material, but has not proved his or her ability to the Association as a genealogist.

Subject Index of Members' Special Interests links to a list of specialisms that include everything from Anglo-Indians to Intestacy to Missionary Records, and House History to University Alumni. Each of these has a code or codes alongside it, and these identify the researchers who specialise in that particular field. Make a note of the relevant codes, therefore, go to the bottom of the page and click on List of Members Available for Commission, and then scroll down to the correct entries. The codes are given alphabetically and then numerically after each name.

Code of Practice outlines what you can expect from an AGRA affiliated researcher.

This is a safe, straightforward route to finding a reliable researcher to help you with your search in whatever field interests you. Total confidentiality is assured.

www.college-of-arms.gov.uk
College of Arms

Overall rating: ★ ★ ★ ★			
Classification: Heraldry		**Readability:**	★ ★ ★ ★ ★
Updating: Regularly		**Content:**	★ ★ ★ ★ ★
Navigation: ★ ★ ★ ★ ★		**Speed:**	★ ★ ★ ★ ★

UK

The College of Arms is the official repository of the coats of arms and pedigrees of England and Wales, and they keep genealogies of the families entitled to bear arms, and are responsible for drawing up new arms. Each officer of arms conducts his own practice in heraldry and genealogy and charges fees to undertake research.

SPECIAL FEATURES

Frequently Asked Questions (on the homepage top tabs or again at the bottom of the page) number only three: Do coats of arms belong to surnames? (The answer is no.) What are the pantone numbers for the colours used in heraldry? What is a crest?

About the College of Arms is the most informative part of the site, within which are found links to The Granting of Arms (number eight in the list) and Having a Coat of Arms or Crest Identified (number eleven).

Enquiries offers an email facility for asking questions.

Links include British Library Manuscript Collections, The British Monarchy – The Official Website, House of Lords Record Office and Royal Commission on Historical Manuscripts.

If you wish to establish a right to a coat of arms, or to identify a coat of arms borne by an ancestor, this is unquestionably the place to come.

www.ihgs.ac.uk
The Institute of Heraldic and Genealogical Studies

Overall rating: ★ ★ ★ ★ ★			
Classification: Heraldry		**Readability:**	★ ★ ★ ★ ★
Updating: Occasionally		**Content:**	★ ★ ★ ★ ★
Navigation: ★ ★ ★ ★		**Speed:**	★ ★ ★ ★ ★

UK

Founded in 1961 by the irrepressible and splendidly-named Cecil Humphery-Smith, the Institute runs courses and tutorial days as well as maintaining a most useful Library that contains 30,000 items, many unique.

SPECIAL FEATURES

The Institute's services fall into three main areas: Heraldic Research (advising on designing and registering new coats of arms and insignia for personal or corporate use); Palaeography (with experts available to interpret, transcribe and translate your old documents, and teach you how to do so yourself); and Handwriting Analysis. The principal is also available to give research advice to anyone with difficulties in their researches. The Institute also assists various medical teams with invaluable genetic research into the hereditary nature of diseases such as Alzheimers and some cancers.

Courses includes a thorough correspondence course (with a few tutorial days) leading to the Institute's Diploma in Genealogy and, at a higher level, Licenciateship of the Institute.

Other sections include **Publications** and **Bookshop, Links** and **Institute Online Diary.** The bookshop has a particularly strong selection, though you cannot order online.

The website of this fine organisation adheres to its standards of excellence and reliability.

www.gendocs.demon.co.uk

GenDocs Genealogical Research in England and Wales

Overall rating: ★ ★ ★ ★			
Classification:	Research	**Readability:**	★ ★ ★ ★
Updating:	Regularly	**Content:**	★ ★ ★ ★
Navigation:	★ ★ ★ ★	**Speed:**	★ ★ ★ ★

UK

John and Elaine Hitchcock, who run this very useful service from their home in Northampton, founded GenDocs in 1992, and have had a website since 1994. They supply genealogical documents worldwide both to private individuals and to research agencies or family history societies. They specialise in English and Welsh ancestry and run a daily courier service in London to all the major archive holdings. They also supply photographs of buildings and monuments in London and the South Midlands. An area of particular personal interest and expertise is Victorian London.

SPECIAL FEATURES

Courier Service, in the left-of-page index, explains that GenDocs will collect copies of documents from The Family Records Centre, London Metropolitan Archives, The Principal Registry of the Family Division, the Guildhall Library and the City of Westminster Archives Centre, though not from the Public Record Office at Kew. Details of charges are available under Courier Prices.

BMD Certificates, Census Returns, Wills & Admons and **Parish Registers** These few items in the index have good, brief explanatory notes, Research Service explains in more detail what GenDocs can do for you.

How to Order explains that orders for documents are only accepted by post and must be prepaid. From this page you can also access the Document Price List. If you would need to travel to London to order documents, this option compares very favourably on cost.

Census Returns for England and Wales 1841-1901 lays out the exact sequence of questions asked in each census, a good guide to what information you can expect if you order a census return for an ancestor at whatever census date.

Information on our other pages The resources listed in the menu on the right-hand side of the page have already been referred to at various points in this book, as their lists, such as Irish Nests, London Metropolitan Police Divisions, London Churches, Cemeteries, Institutions, Inns, Taverns and Public Houses, and Census Indexes are essential materials for anyone researching Victorian London.

Glossaries These are two very useful features located in the right-of-page yellow boxes. One explains abbreviations and acronyms commonly found in genealogy, the other the meanings of the names of ranks, trades and professions.

This could be an extremely useful service for those not able to get to London to pursue research but who have identified the documents they want, and a site that is definitely worth visiting even if you are not planning on engaging their services.

www.ukancestors.info/index.htm

UK Ancestors

★ ★ ★ ★   UK

London-based Paul Blake is a well-qualified genealogical researcher, lecturer and contributor to *Family History Monthly* and other magazines.

www.kenaud.dircon.co.uk
Audrey Collins BA

★★★★ UK

This experienced researcher has much knowledge of London and Middlesex, and has written books published by the FFHS about Using the Family Records Centre, and Basic Facts about Using Wills from 1858, among others. She specialises in census searches, parish register searches, and newspaper searches, and on the site there is good information about what information these records contain. The site clearly sets out the terms of engagement and what you can expect for the fees. Payment is also accepted in Australian dollars.

www.brit-a-r.demon.co.uk
British Ancestral Research

★★★★ UK

Tim Cooper is a private reseacher offering a one-price service and guaranteeing to trace two names back at least four generations (or partial money back).

www.genfindit.com
Genfindit

★★★★ UK

This is an online ordering service for copies of English, Welsh, Scottish, Irish, Australian and New Zealand vital records, including BDMs, wills and census returns. They will help with one-name studies, extracting all occurrences of names from specified sources. Further records, such as Irish Church Parish Registers, are being added to their list regularly.

www.research-uk.com
Research UK

★★★★ UK

With so many useful links on the homepage it can be difficult to identify the ones that actually tell you about the services of this reliable company. Look for BMDs, Census Search, Wills and Divorces. You can order searches online, and pay by credit card on secure servers, or pay by post if you prefer. They will also undertake to trace people for non-genealogical purposes.

www.yorkshireancestors.com
Yorkshire Ancestors

★★★★ UK

Not exactly a research service, but if you are planning a trip to Yorkshire, this would be a good place to stay. They offer bed and breakfast and self-catering accommodation in a Victorian farmhouse within easy drive of the record offices of York, Beverley and Northallerton. The added bonus is use of the small but well equipped Yorkshire Family History Research Library on site, where assistance and advice on getting started is also offered.

www.ancestors.co.uk/index.html
Ancestors of Dover Ltd

★★★★ UK

To discover how this service works consult Questions in the grey bar. The money-back guarantee is an attractive feature and a good deal of internal information is available from these pages, though presented in a rather 'bitty' form.

useful addresses

The British Library
96 Euston Road
London
NW1 2DB
tel: 020 7412 7676
email: reader-services-enquiries@bl.uk

Corporation of London Library and Art Gallery
(COLLAGE)
PO Box 270
Guildhall
London
EC2P 2EJ
tel: 020 7332 3097
email: pro@corpoflondon.gov.uk

Dr Williams's Library
14 Gordon Square
London
WC1H 0AG
tel: 020 7387 3727
fax: 020 7388 1142
email: 101340.2541@compuserve.com

Family Records Centre
1 Myddelton Street
London
EC1R 1UW
BMDs tel: 0870 243 7788 fax: 01704 550013
email: certificate.services@ons.gov.uk
Census and general enquiries tel: 020 8392 5300
fax: 020 8392 5307
email: enquiry@pro.gov.uk

Federation of Family History Societies
PO Box 2425
Coventry
CV5 6YX
tel: 01704 149 032

General Register Office
PO Box 2
Southport
Merseyside
PR8 2JD

general information: 0151 471 4800
email: certificate.services@ons.gov.uk

The Guild of One-Name Studies
Box G
14 Charterhouse Buildings
Goswell Road
London
EC1M 7BA

email: guild@one-name.org

Guildhall Library
Aldermanbury
London
EC2P 2EJ

tel: manuscript section 020 7332 1862/1863
email: manuscripts.guildhall@corpoflondon.gov.uk

maps and prints: 020 7332 1839
email: prints&maps@corpoflondon.gov.uk
printed books: 020 7332 1868/1870
email: printedbooks.guildhall@corpoflondon.gov.uk

bookshop: 020 7332 1858
fax: 020 7600 3384
email: bookshop@corpoflondon.gov.uk

Historical Manuscripts, Commission
Quality House
Quality Court
Chancery Lane
London WC2A 1HP

tel: 020 7242 1198
fax: 020 7831 3550
email: nra@hmc.gov.uk

LDS Distribution Centre
399 Garretts Green Lane
Birmingham
B33 0UH
tel: 0870 010 2051
fax: 0870 010 2052

London Metropolitan Archives
40 Northhampton Road
London Ec1R OHB
tel: 020 7332 3820
fax: 020 7833 9136
email: ask.lma@corpoflondon.gov.uk

Office For National Statistics, see General
Register Office

The Public Record Office
Kew
Richmond
Surrey
TW9 4DU

tel: 020 8876 3444
fax: 020 8392 5286

The Society of Genealogists
14 Charterhouse Buildings
Goswell Road
London
EC1M 7BA

tel: 020 7251 8799
fax: 020 7250 1800

commonly used acronyms

afsd	aforesaid
AGRA	Association of Genealogists and Researchers in Archives
b.o.t.p.	both of this parish
bach	bachelor
BMDs	Births, marriages and deaths. Also known as Vital Records.
BT	Bishops Transcripts, copies of parish records lodged with the archdiocese. Also known as Parish Register Transcripts
d.	died
dau.	daughter
daur	daughter (often used on census returns)
FHC	Family History Centre; collections of research resources run by the Latter Day Saints.
FHL	Family History Library; the huge Mormon repository in Salt Lake City, Utah
FHS	Family History Societies
FRC	Family Records Centre, in Myddleton Street, London. The successor of Somerset House and St Catherine's House as the repository of BMD indexes, known as GRO indexes.
GEDCOM	Genealogical Data Communication; a standard file format for the transfer of genealogical data.
GRO	General Records Office
GRONI	General Records Office of Northern Ireland
IGI	International Genealogy Index
LDS	Latter Day Saints, also known as Mormons. See p. 36
LMA	London Metropolitan Archives
NBI	National Burial Index; an index of death records produced by the FHHS as a complement to the IGI which ignores burial records. Available on CDs.
newbie	someone new to family history or a particular mailing list
ONS	Office of National Statistics. Government office responsible for the census and issuing certificates of BDMs.
PAF	Personal Ancestral File; a free LDS family history software program.
PDF	Portable Document Format; a popular file format created by Adobe for offline reading of reports and documents which can be read by anyone with the free program Acrobat Reader.
PRO	Public Records Office, based at Kew
PRONI	Public Records Office of Norther Ireland
PRT	parish register transcripts
SKS	in email: some kind soul
SOG	Society of Genealogists
TIA	in email: thanks in advance
URL	Uniform Resource Locator; an internet address, usually starting with http:// or www.

using the website

The Good Web Guide
www.thegoodwebguide.co.uk

The Good Web Guide provides simple one-click access to all the sites mentioned in this book, and is an easy way to start exploring the internet. All books about the internet become slightly out of date as soon they're printed, but with the free updates you'll receive as a subscriber to the Good Web Guide website, this book will remain current as long as you're a member.

The goodwebguide.co.uk homepage provides links to each of the GWG subject channels, including Genealogy. It also lists headlines and links to some of the newest articles, reviews and competitions on the site, and details of special offers on other Good Web Guide books.

Although some reviews and articles are free to view, the majority of the content on the Good Web Guide site is accessible only to members. Begin by clicking on the small 'Register Now' icon near the top left of the page. When you've filled in and submitted your details a menu will appear on the left of the page. Choose the option Register a Purchase. A list of questions will appear, but you only need to answer the one relevant to this book, and you will need to have the book in front of you to find the answer. Once you're registered you'll be able to view the contents of this book online, and be eligible for free updates. As a member you can upgrade to obtain access to all the channels at a specially discounted rate.

Reviews are organised by chapter, with the new reviews in the Latest Additions section. At the bottom of each review there is a link straight to the site, so you don't have to worry about typing in the addresses. New reviews are added at least monthly, sometimes weekly. You can also sign up for free newsletters to have website reviews delivered straight to your desk.

index

Methodist Minister and
 Probationers 122
metropolitan, see London
 Metropolitan Police Divisions
Mexico 36, 108
Mick Gray 125
microfiche and microfilm 41-43,
 45, 55, 59, 81, 107, 114, 126
 for purchase 59, 85, 114, 126,
 148, 155
 readers 161
Middlesex 79, 172
migration 28, 32, 33, 51, 65, 67,
 81-84, 87, 92-104, 112, 117, 128,
 132, 134
 surname 52
Militaria on the Web 129
military 34, 77, 92, 95, 98,
 104, 123-129, 132, 134, 155,
 156
 air force 129
 army 17, 41, 105, 112, 127
 merchant navy 128
 navy 17, 60, 112, 126, 128
 world wars 124-126, 156, 168
 see also war memorials
Military Badges 130
Military Heritage 130
military images 130
militia, see military
ministers 122
Ministry of Defence, the 123, 127,
 128
 veterans' agency 124
 see also military
Minneapolis 81
missions 121, 169
misreadings and mistakes, see
 transcription, spelling variants
missing persons, finding 126, 135,
 172
MOD, see Ministry of Defence
Modern Records Centre 113
monarchy, see royalty
money 134, 145
monuments 133, 171
 see also cemeteries, war
 memorials
Moravians 132
Morgan, George G 158
Mormon Index, see International
 Genealogical Index
Mormons, see Church of Jesus

Christ of the Latter Day Saints
MultiMap 74, 138
Mumford, Bill 158
Munich 168
Murray, Sabina J. 136
museums 29, 42, 48, 126, 128
music halls 113
MW Microfilm Supplies 161
MyFamily.com 54

names;
 one-name studies 52, 68, 70, 74,
 87, 135, 160, 172
 searches 11, 51-71, 81, 85, 132
 see also surnames
Namibia 95
naming patterns 132
NAS, see National Archives of
 Scotland
national archives 132
National Archives of Ireland 80
National Archives of Norway 104
National Archives of Scotland 43, 86
National Burials Index, the 41, 59
National Digital Archive of Datasets
 44
National Federation of Cemetery
 Friends 133
National Inventory of War Memorials
 41
National Library of Ireland 81
National Library of Scotland 86
National Library of Wales 88
National Maritime Museum, the
 128
National Monuments Record 133
National Monuments Record of
 Scotland, the 133
National Register of Archives, the
 48
National Strays Index, the 41
natural parents, see adoption
navigation, see advice
navy, see military
NBI, see National Burials Index
NCVCCO 117
Neep, Rod 156
Netherlands, the 103
Netserf: the Internet connection for
 Medieval Resources 141
newbies, see newcomers
Newbies Helping Newbies 23

newcomers 32, 38, 96, 145
 see also advice
Newgate Prison 114
Newington 76
Newman, Paul 113
newsgroups 39, 40
newsletters 142
 see also publications
New South Wales 23, 97
Newspaper Library Catalogue, the
 143
newspapers 54, 64, 78, 98, 107, 143,
 162, 163
 Ireland 81
 searches 172
newsreading software 39
news servers 39, 40
New to Family History 152
New York 109
New Zealand 57, 65, 92, 117, 172
Nigeria 95
NISRA, see Northern Ireland
 Statistics and Research Agency
nobility 11, 41, 118, 119, 168
Nonconformists 58, 122
Norfolk 59, 63, 151
Northallerton 172
North America, see United States
Northampton 171
Northern Ireland Genealogy 83, 84
Northern Ireland Statistics and
 Research Agency 84
Northgate, Canterbury 168
North Middlesex 79
Norway 104
Norwich 151
Notes and Queries 143
novices, see newcomers
NRA, see National Register of
 Archives
numbers 136, 137
 see also batch numbers
nurses 112, 117
 see also records, hospital and
 medical
Nursing, history of 117
NZ, see New Zealand

obituaries 51, 64, 65
Obituary Archive Search Engine 64
Obituary Daily Times, the 64
Observer, the 64
Obsolete Occupations 112

occupations 41, 47, 52, 55, 60, 105,
 107, 112, 113, 132, 134
Odin's Castle of Dreams and
 Legends 141
O'Donovan, J 160
offences, see criminals
Office of National Statistics, the 43,
 45, 55, 88
O'Hara, Bob 126
Ohio Public Library 35
Old English commodity measures
 145
older members of the family 16
Old Handwriting 136
Old-maps.co.uk 139
old ordnance survey maps 163
Old Occupations Names Index 112
Olive Tree Genealogy 65, 109
one-name studies, see names
online;
 communities, see message boards
 navigation, see advice
 purchasing 147-165, 172
Online Latin-English/English-Latin
 Dictionary, the 137
Online Medical Dictionary, the 140
Online Resource Book for Medieval
 Studies 141
Online Study Group for Irish
 Genealogy 82
ONS, see Office of National
 Statistics
operating systems, see advice
ORB, see Online Resource Book for
 Medieval Studies
ordering, see online, purchasing
orders;
 military 129
 religious 121
Ordnance Survey 138, 139, 163,
 164
 see also maps
Ordnance Survey Get-a-map 138
original documents, see sources,
 primary
Origins.net 31
orphans and orphanages, see poor
 people
Ottawa 99
Our Timelines 160
overseas, see records, international

Familia

Familia is a web-based directory of family history resources held in public libraries in the UK and Ireland, to guide you quickly to the information you require.

Familia is a great place to begin your research and includes advice and clear analysis of local history collections across the country with details of where to find:

- Census Returns
- Directories and Registers
- Local History Periodicals
- Indexes of Births, Marriages and Deaths

Find us at : **http://www.familia.org.uk**

Managed by

NGfL

King or Commoner?
Hanged or Knighted?

Who were your ancestors?

**Let Britain's leading genealogists
discover your family history.**

**For a free estimate and brochure
contact:**

*Achievements
of Canterbury*

Centre for Heraldic and Genealogical Research and Artwork
Northgate, Canterbury, Kent, CT1 1BA
Tel 01227 462618 Fax 01227 765617 Web www.achievements.co.uk
Email achievements@achievements.co.uk

THE ASSOCIATION OF GENEALOGISTS AND RESEARCHERS IN ARCHIVES

Formerly The Association of Genealogists and Record Agents

Research

For assistance in all areas of British family history choose an expert from the List of Members.

£2.50 (UK) or 6 IRCs (overseas)

Membership

Membership of AGRA is open to those who can provide evidence of a high level of competence and professional experience.

website: www.agra.org.uk

Enquiries to:
The Secretaries
29 Badgers Close
Horsham
W. Sussex RH12 5RU

Founded 1968
Incorporated 1998
A Code of Practice is in force

BACK TO ROOTS (UK) LTD, 16 Arrowsmith Drive, Stonehouse, GL10 2QR
www.backtoroots.co.uk Tel: 01453 821300

Family Tree Maker V9 1-CD Set	£29.95
Family Tree Maker V9 Upgrade	£19.95
(p&p on FTM packages £1.00)	
Full range of Family Tree Maker CDs in stock	
Generations Grande Suite V8 UK	£44.00
Generations Starter Kit V8	£26.00
(p&p on Generations packages £3.50)	
Generations Essentials (p&p £1.50)	£12.95
Family Origins V10 (p&p £1.50)	£34.00
Family Origins V10 Upgrade (p&p 75p)	£19.00
LDS Companion (p&p £1)	£16.50

Data CDs - (p&p 75p ea.)

National Burial Index	£30.00
1891 Census for London (38 CDs)	£49.95
1851 Census for Gloucestershire, Bristol & Somerset	£15.00
Marylebone 1821 & 1831 Census (Surname Index)	£10.50
Criminal Registers 1805-1816 (every county in England & Wales)	£11.99 ea.
Muster Rolls 1781-82 (All Counties)	£3.99 ea.

Hundreds more items in stock please refer to webpage or send for free brochure.

Data CDs - (p&p 75p ea.)

Over 100 Kelly's & Pigot's Street & Trade Directories on CD - £11.99 each - e.g.

Berkshire Kelly's 1911 Alphabetical list of Private Residents & Trade Directory

City of Gloucester & District Smart's 1920 Street & Private Residents Directory

West Kensington & Hammersmith, Shepherds Bush & Fulham Kelly's 1898-99 Street & Private Residents Directory

Harrow including Wealdstone, Wembley, Sudbury, Northwood & Pinner Kelly's 1919-20 Street, Private Residents & Trade Dir

Acid Free Products

Certificate Binders (Standard) in red, green & black (p&p £2.50)	£9.90
Certificate Binders (Deluxe) in burgundy, cedar green & blue (p&p £2.50)	£13.50
Polypockets for Certificate Binders	55p ea.
Insert Cards (pk of 10) (p&p 50p/pk)	£2.90
Dividers (pk of 5) (p&p 50p/pk)	£2.60
Photo/Memorabilia Album in burgundy, cedar green & blue (p&p £1.00)	£6.60
Polypockets for photo album C1 (A4), C2 (A4 - 2 divisions) C4 (A4 - 4 division)	45p ea.
(p&p multiples of 10 polypockets 50p ea.)	

other great titles in thegoodwebguide series:

paperback   £7.99/£8.99

book lovers .... ISBN 1-903282-42-x
food .... ISBN 1-903282-17-9
gardening .... ISBN 1-903282-16-0
parents .... ISBN 1-903282-19-5
property .... ISBN 1-903282-44-6
the good web guide: .... ISBN 1-903282-46-2
2nd edition

hardback   £12.99

antiques and collectables .... ISBN 1-903282-21-7
home and interiors .... ISBN 1-903282-15-2
museums and galleries .... ISBN 1-903282-14-4
world religions .... ISBN 1-903282-25-x

small paperbacks   £4.99

comedy .... ISBN 1-903282-20-9
gay life .... ISBN 1-903282-13-6
holiday travel online .... ISBN 1-903282-32-2
mind, body and spirit .... ISBN 1-903282-40-3
sport .... ISBN 1-903282-07-1
tracing your family history .... ISBN 1-903282-33-0
tv .... ISBN 1-903282-12-8

mini paperbacks   £2.50

chocolate .... ISBN 1-903282-34-9
conspiracies .... ISBN 1-903282-36-5